# THE BOY
# WHO NEVER
# CAME HOME

# THE BOY WHO NEVER CAME HOME

## THE INSIDE STORY OF MISSING TEENAGER PHILIP CAIRNS

### EMMA McMENAMY

mB

MIRROR BOOKS

Author Emma McMenamy is an established news and crime journalist who currently works as chief reporter with the *Irish Sunday Mirror.*

With over two decades working for national newspaper titles, she has broken many exclusive investigative stories including on the disappearance of schoolboy Philip Cairns.

She has also been nominated for awards, including Crime Reporter of the Year.

*Dedicated to Philip,*
*his loving family,*
*and all those who are missing*
*who never came home.*

m
B

MIRROR BOOKS

1

Published in Great Britain and Ireland in 2021 by
Mirror Books, a Reach PLC business,
5 St Paul's Square, Liverpool, L3 9SJ.

www.mirrorbooks.co.uk
@TheMirrorBooks

ISBN: 9781913406752
eBook ISBN: 9781913406769

Photographic acknowledgements:
Collins, PA/Alamy, RTÉ Archive, Nikita Cooke, Mirrorpix.
Every effort has been made to trace copyright. Any omissions or oversights
will be rectified in future editions.

Design and production by Mirror Books.

Printed and bound by CPI Group (UK) Ltd,
Croydon, CR0 4YY.

# Contents

# Introduction

In 1986, Ireland was a far cry from the country we now see. A sense of innocence filled the air, young children played unaccompanied with their friends for hours on the streets and front doors were left unlocked. People hitch-hiked on the side of the road and young kids walked to and from school on their own.

It was, perhaps, part ignorance, but the public at large generally felt very safe. Chris De Burgh's 'Lady in Red' filled the airwaves that summer while the country was still mourning the sudden death of Thin Lizzy frontman Phil Lynott that January.

It was a year which marked many historic Irish events too. The troubles in the North were simmering, anti-divorce protests were taking place, Hurricane Charley battered the country, the 20p coin was introduced into circulation and Jack Charlton took over as the new Ireland football manager.

It was also the year the country's most infamous art heist took place when a gang of 13 criminals, led by notorious Dublin gangster Martin "The General" Cahill, were involved in the biggest theft of priceless paintings in the State's history. The gang escaped with a haul of 18 masterpieces, including some of the most valuable by Goya and Vermeer, from the

Beit collection at Russborough House in Co Wicklow. At the time the collection was estimated to be worth in the region of IR£30 million.

But there was one event, arguably more than any other in 1986, which stopped people in their tracks and brought the whole country to a standstill. One which still lingers in many people's minds right up to the present day – the disappearance of Dublin schoolboy Philip Cairns.

On the afternoon of October 23, the teenager finished eating his lunch at his family home in Rathfarnham, packed his books into his schoolbag ahead of his afternoon classes, and set off for his ten-minute journey back to Colaiste Eanna. As he left the family's semi-detached house on Ballyroan Road he shouted back to his grandmother May, "Cheerio, Gran. I'm off." It would be the last time Philip's voice would ever be heard.

The happy teenager, who had only just started secondary school seven weeks earlier, never made it back to class after his lunch break and what happened to him after he stepped foot outside his front door remains a mystery right up until the present day. There have been many theories over the years as to what may have happened to Philip but none have ever been able to be stood up. They range from plausible hypotheses to downright outlandish crazy speculations.

This year sees the 35th anniversary of his disappearance. During that time, Philip's heartbroken parents, Alice and his late father Philip Snr, as well as his four sisters, Mary, Sandra, Suzanne and Helen and younger brother Eoin, have never given up searching for him. Their determination to find out the truth has never wavered.

His family firmly believe that he did not run away from them. There is the possibility he was involved in an accident on route back to school but proof has never emerged to back this claim up and Philip would never have mitched off school, according to his mother Alice many years ago. It just wasn't in him.

For the family, the abduction theory is the most plausible. But as his late father Philip Snr once said, he would never have got into a car with a stranger. So did he get picked up along the busy Ballyroan Road by someone he knew or recognised?

And while it is highly believed that the teenager may have been killed by his kidnapper, the absence of a crime scene or the teenager's remains means gardaí are still treating his disappearance as a missing persons case.

I first became aware of Philip's disappearance and the mystery which surrounded it when I embarked on a career in journalism 20 years ago. Over the years working as a crime reporter, I covered many intriguing, sad and at times terrifying stories. But of them all, Philip's case stuck with me. It baffled me how a well-behaved teenager could disappear on a busy Dublin street, never to be seen again.

As the mother of a young son myself I cannot begin to imagine the pain his mother and late father have had to endure, living every parent's worst nightmare, day after day, year after year. I met with two of Philip's sisters during the course of writing this book. They were two of the nicest, most humble people I have ever met.

On top of the hurt they are already suffering, they have also had to contend with years of malicious rumours about what might have possibly happened to the teenager. They include unfounded speculation that he was abducted by a religious cult or murdered by a local paedophile ring. For me, meeting Philip's sisters and the way they accommodated me despite the devastating heartache they still suffer, only made me more determined to try and find out the truth.

Detectives have shown an unswerving determination to bring some closure to the case for the long-suffering family. They have worked tirelessly to try and establish what happened to the 13-year-old, leaving no stone unturned. No other children were abducted from the area before or after Philip's case, leading many investigators to believe it was a one-off incident, perhaps carried out by somebody known and trusted by the teenager. Detectives agree with the family that the likelihood of Philip being involved in an accident or running away from home are highly unlikely. They are of the firm belief that, sadly, something sinister may have happened to the caring young boy on the day he disappeared.

Former Detective Sergeant Tom Doyle devoted 18 years of his career in trying to find out what happened to the schoolboy. I have spoken to him at length, as well as other detectives who worked on the early investigation. For Doyle, 2016 was a key year when it emerged that a prolific paedophile by the name of Eamon Cooke was a person of interest.

I extensively covered this developing story for the *Irish Daily Mirror*. Along with the whole country, I waited with bated breath to find out if gardaí at the time were able to link him to one of Ireland's longest unsolved missing person cases. Yet, due to a lack of evidence, investigating officers could not conclusively determine whether he was involved or not.

Cooke, who was serving a lengthy sentence for child abuse

at the time, was in a hospice dying from lung cancer. When a woman, who was a victim of the child abuser, came forward and signed a statement claiming she had seen the pirate radio DJ hitting the teenager over the head at his Radio Dublin studio, detectives thought they had their breakthrough.

They faced a race against time to determine whether the woman's account was plausible. Investigating officers quizzed the abuser and according to former Detective Sergeant Tom Doyle, Cooke gave answers which sent chills down his spine. He told me: "We interviewed him and planned to take it further and then we learnt that he had passed away. At one stage we did think he was going to confess and tell us what he knew."

This book reopens the investigation into Cooke. Over the course of a year I have delved into the past to try and determine if in fact he did have a key role to play in Philip's disappearance. In doing so, I believe I have unearthed critical new information pertaining to the chief suspect which could prove highly beneficial to investigating officers. I have shared these details with Philip's family as well as the gardaí and I hope that they will help detectives with their investigation.

The teenager's schoolbag remains the only evidence that exists in the case. Six days after Philip went missing, his grey satchel was found in a laneway just 400 metres away from his home. To this day, nobody has come forward claiming to have placed the bag there. For many officers working on the case, they believe this piece of evidence may hold the key to solving the mystery.

One of the teenage girls who discovered the bag, Catherine Hassett, recalled to me how, along with her friend Orla O'Carroll, they stumbled across it while on their way to a

# THE BOY WHO NEVER CAME HOME

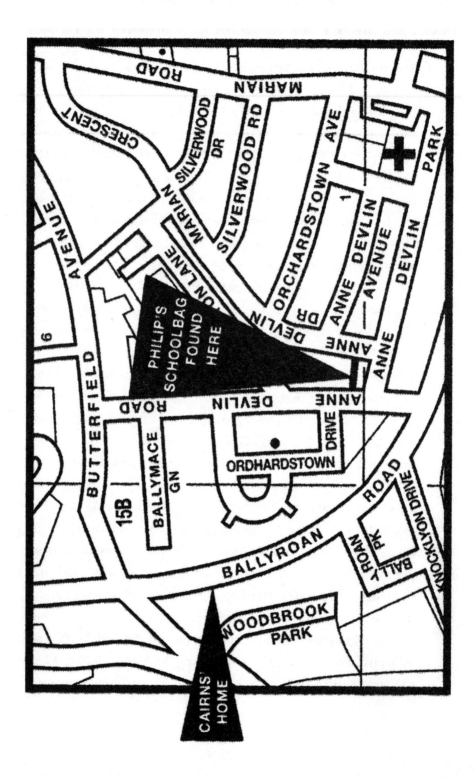

friend's house. Speaking for the first time in 35 years, Catherine said the pals were terrified that the person who had left the bag back in the narrow laneway may have been still lurking close by.

While samples taken from Cooke reportedly did not match DNA on Philip's schoolbag, according to many it does not mean he was not involved. As former cold case detective Alan Bailey pointed out, perhaps the child abuser didn't touch the schoolbag. There is also the possibility that his DNA is within the mixed samples which Irish scientists have not yet been able to extract single profiles from.

A top American DNA expert, Dr Mark Perlin, said his company has the technology to determine if this is the case. The world-renowned specialist believes his Pittsburg-based Cybergenetics team could finally help to conclusively determine whether Cooke did touch the bag or not by testing the complex samples using technology he has developed.

There is also the possibility that the paedophile was not involved in Philip's abduction, despite one detective telling me that he believes he's the number one suspect. It would be foolish to pin all suspicion on Cooke as there is the chance that someone else was involved in the long-standing unsolved case. What if it was someone who, up until now, has managed to stay below the Garda radar? Or what if one of those who gave a statement to officers over the many years secretly holds the key to solving the case?

Forensic psychologists and criminologists play a huge role in helping investigators to determine what may have happened on the day of a specific crime. They are also relied upon to give a profile of the perpetrator.

I have called on two renowned experts in their field to try to establish what may have happened to the schoolboy and what kind of person his suspected kidnapper could have been. One of the world's most renowned forensic psychologists, Dr Julian Boon, and top Irish criminologist Professor John O'Keeffe, both give their expert opinions on the case.

Sadly, Philip's disappearance is just one of many missing person cases in Ireland. Close to 9,000 people are reported missing by loved ones each year. However, only a small number of children like the teenager disappear, never to be seen again.

There is the tragic case of little six-year-old Mary Boyle in Donegal, who vanished in 1977. Her heartbroken family including her twin sister Ann, have never given up hope of finding her and like Philip's devastated family, just want to be able to bring her home and give her a proper burial. Ann told me how her sister is always on her mind and that she hopes to one day find out what happened to her bubbly sibling on the day she went missing.

There's also the unsolved abduction and murder of Bernadette Connolly in Co Sligo in 1970. To date, nobody has been charged over her kidnapping and brutal killing. Both investigations sadly remain unsolved.

Philip's high-profile case, which has never been far from the news headlines, continues to pull on the heartstrings of the public. But behind the many news stories is a family who have had to endure years of pain not knowing what happened to their loved one.

Former Detective Sergeant Tom Doyle has never stopped thinking about the case, despite retiring from the force a number of years ago.

# INTRODUCTION

It saddens him that despite their best efforts, he never found out what happened to the teenager on that fateful day. All he can do is hope that someday someone will find it within their heart to come forward with the information the family so desperately needs to help bring their boy home.

"Philip Cairns left home after his lunch to return to school. He was never seen again. The public are reminded of the case from time to time in an effort to encourage people with information to come forward. However, the family of Philip are reminded on a daily basis by the absence of their loved one.

"More than anything, Philip's mother and siblings want to know what happened to him, to their loved one, to their boy who never came home."

# 1.

# The Day

*'He fully intended to go back to school and was not the type to talk to strangers or wander off'*

On Thursday, October 23, 1986, schoolboy Philip Cairns set off on his half-mile journey to school. It was a typical cold and blustery autumn morning. The 13-year-old had just started his first year at local all-boys secondary school, Colaiste Eanna in Rathfarnham, Co Dublin. The five-foot teenager, who had an innocent look which made him appear younger than his years, had almost completed his seventh week at his new school. "He was delighted with it and happy and able to cope," his mother Alice said.

Following his morning classes, the softly-spoken and well-behaved teenager made the short ten-minute walk back to the family's suburban home on Ballyroan Road at 12.45pm.

His new secondary school routine saw him returning for his hour-long lunch break. Philip liked routine and according to his father Philip Snr, he was so regular in his movements that you could have set your watch to him. He was a very happy boy who was also very thoughtful and kind and got on with everyone, according to those who knew him. A far cry from the distressed and vulnerable loner some people would inaccurately describe him as years later. In fact, Philip was a typical teenager without a care in the world. He was starting to show more interest in things that mattered to boys his age like music, having a cool hairstyle and clothes. He was also very religious and regularly attended mass, often accompanying his mother to weekly devotions to Our Lady of Fatima.

Philip's favourite pastimes included going fishing with his father and kicking a football around with his younger brother Eoin, who was just 14 months his junior. "We'd have these ridiculously long football competitions," Eoin said years later. "We had an interest in sea fishing. My father was a member of Dublin Sea Angling Club and Philip was very interested in it. Philip loved that, he was great fun to be around."

After returning home at lunchtime, Philip talked to his granny May, who was living with the Cairns family at the time, and ate a sandwich before doing some maths homework and getting his school books ready for his afternoon classes. His mother Alice said he was keen to please and always tried his best when it came to his school work. "He wouldn't have been a brilliant pupil I'd say, but he listened and he got on much better in the last couple of years, he had a great teacher."

The teen came from a very stable home where he lived with his loving parents, granny and his four sisters, Mary, Sandra,

Helen, Suzanne and younger brother Eoin. He was extremely close to Eoin, who he shared a bedroom with.

It was just like any other day at the Cairns household except Helen had stayed off school with a terrible toothache. It had been getting progressively worse over the course of a few days. Alice was getting ready to take Helen into the dental hospital in Dublin city centre as the local dentist was away. Suzanne was also in the house.

Amid the commotion, Philip sorted out the schoolbooks he needed for that afternoon's lessons in religion, maths and geography. After almost two months at his new school, he was starting to remember what classes he had each day. He kept an eye on the clock and at 1.20pm he put his bag on his back and left for his return journey to school. There was nothing out of the ordinary and Philip's demeanour seemed the same as usual.

The caring teen had volunteered to stay back to mind his grandmother but Alice opted for his sister Suzanne, who was 15 at the time, to do that job instead. With that he headed into the hall and called out, "Cheerio, Gran. I'm off," before closing the front door behind him. Nobody saw him leave.

It would be the last time his voice would ever be heard.

Normally, his mother would stand at the gate and watch her son walk up the road towards the school but she didn't on this particular day as she was too busy getting ready to head to the dentist with Helen. As far as Philip's family were concerned, he had returned to school that afternoon. "I was in the kitchen and took it for granted he had gone back to school," his mother Alice said in the days that followed. "I said to myself, 'He's a big boy now.'"

Meanwhile, his teachers at Colaiste Eanna assumed Philip had failed to return that afternoon due to a family emergency or because he had fallen sick. He never missed school, so they were the most plausible explanations.

At around 5pm that evening, Philip Snr returned home from his job at Nestlé and there was no sign of his eldest son. Initially he wasn't too worried and assumed Philip, who was still settling in and getting to grips with his new school routine, had perhaps decided to play with some of his friends before returning home.

Usually the teen was at the family's semi-detached house from school by 4.15pm on the button. It was only when his mother returned with Helen from the dentist that evening and the teenager still wasn't home that panic began to set in.

She asked her other children if they had seen or heard from their sibling or knew where he was. "We said we didn't know, we didn't see him. She was a little bit anxious really, thinking, 'well, that's not really like Philip, usually he would check in and say where he was going,'" Philip's brother Eoin would later recall, adding it was totally out of character for him to go "off on a whim".

Alice's motherly instinct kicked in and she decided to check with her missing son's friends to see if they had seen him earlier that day.

Philip was due to swing by and pick up his friend Dean Dowling en route back to school so they could walk back together. But it would later emerge that the two friends' paths never crossed that afternoon. Alice went around to the house of Philip's best friend Enda Cloke to see if he was there, but the schoolboy wasn't. In fact, none of his close pals had seen him that afternoon. His mother would soon learn from his pals as well as his teachers that the teenager had never returned to school following his lunch break. This was totally out of character for Philip and fear quickly crept in.

It was cold that evening and, being late October, it had started to get dark early. As concern grew for the boy's welfare, neighbour Paddy Cloke – Enda's father, who was also a guard – called Rathfarnham Garda Station at 6.30pm to report the youngster missing.

Within hours his panic-stricken family, concerned neighbours and local Garda officers were out searching for the boy. His mother Alice said: "He fully intended to go back to school that day and was not the type to talk to strangers or wander off. He loved to be at home with his family and always came home from school on time."

Little did his mother realise that just minutes after leaving the safety of his family home, her little boy Philip would vanish without a trace never to be seen again.

His disappearance has continued to haunt his family, the public and gardaí ever since. It launched an investigation which has spanned 35 years and remains open to this day.

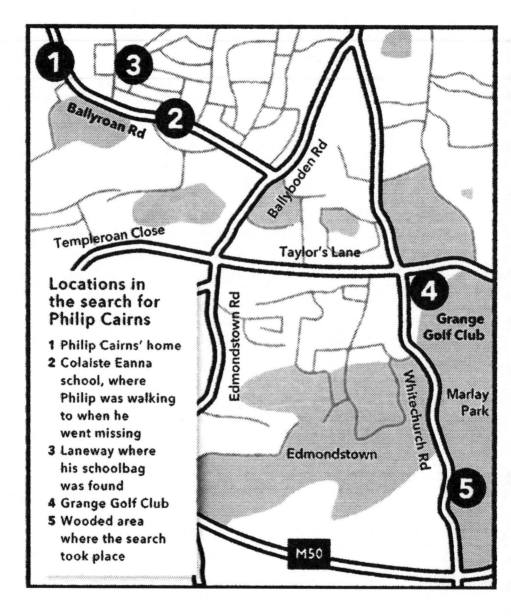

**Locations in the search for Philip Cairns**

1 Philip Cairns' home
2 Colaiste Eanna school, where Philip was walking to when he went missing
3 Laneway where his schoolbag was found
4 Grange Golf Club
5 Wooded area where the search took place

# 2.

# The Hunt

*'We hope you will come home soon.
Don't be worried about anything, we
just want you to come home'*

Due to the schoolboy's age and the bad weather, it was decided by a Garda inspector, who had called to the Cairns family home after he was reported missing, to put out a full alert and call in officers from nearby stations to begin a full-scale search immediately. Guards as well as neighbours and friends of the respected family took part.

The Cairns family, who had lived on Ballyroan Road since the late 1970s after moving from St Columba's Road, Drumcondra, were very well liked and locals did everything they possibly could in the days that followed to try to help find Philip. But the teen was nowhere to be seen, he had literally disappeared without a trace.

There was the possibility that he could have wandered off somewhere by himself but that was quickly ruled out as the hours passed. Plus, the £40 he had saved in a building society also remained untouched. Surely if he planned to leave that day he would have withdrawn the money as he would have needed it to live off? Nothing about the scenario screamed a tearaway teen, and Philip's family and officers investigating the case knew it.

Gardaí at the time were still treating the disappearance as another missing child case, one of the many hundreds they received each year. But Philip's disappearance was different in that the vast majority of those who had gone missing that year had returned home after just a night or two. Inspector Pat King said at the time: "We're still treating it as a missing person case but his disappearance is totally inconsistent with the boy's character. This was a quiet young boy, very regular in his habits. He had a good relationship with his family and went fishing with his father."

The nearest thing the gardaí got to a lead during the initial few days of the investigation was a report by a woman who said she had picked up a child fitting Philip's description in Kilshenane, Co Tipperary. She claimed the boy said he was from Co Waterford and had slept in a guest house but the woman had formed the impression he was sleeping rough. But detectives' confidence in finding the boy safe and well and returning him to his parents were quickly dashed when they tracked down the boy in question and it transpired that it was not the missing teen.

The boy's father also said they had checked with their wider family to see if he was with them. Philip's mother Alice is originally from Kilkenny and she had also asked if the boy had turned up on their doorstep. His father said: "He hasn't been with any relatives or friends. My feelings are that he wasn't a child to run away. The only thing I can think of is that someone or somebody must have, by way of coercion or trickery, taken him."

Three days after he vanished, on October Bank Holiday Sunday, Philip Snr reiterated just how happy the schoolboy was before going missing and how the family were becoming increasingly more concerned about his safety. His father made a desperate appeal to the public for information surrounding his son's whereabouts. "It's now over 48 hours and if anyone can help trace him, please do." All his devastated family could do was sit and wait, hoping and praying that they would receive a call to say he had been found safe and well. Unfortunately, the call never came and the days quickly crept by without any sign of the teenager.

A black and white picture of Philip was placed in the windows of every local shop and business in the hope that the smiling image of the boy in his confirmation outfit would jog someone's memory of having seen him.

His worried mother, not wanting to think the worst, even made a direct appeal to her eldest boy, pleading with him if he had run away to not worry and return home. The mother-of-six refused to give up hope of finding her little boy. "We hope you will come home soon, don't be worried about anything, we just want you home."

After a number of days and with the Garda investigation continuing to hit dead ends, Philip's disappearance started to gain a lot of traction in the national media and his photograph began to appear on the front page of every newspaper. Philip's heartbroken parents continued to appeal to the public for help in finding their boy as they tried to come to terms with what had just happened. They had gone from living a happy normal life to being catapulted into the middle of a media storm.

Local parents now also feared for their own children's safety and many kids were not allowed to continue their daily routine of walking to and from the nearby schools. Panic had crept into every household that there was a child snatcher on the loose and that no youngster was safe. There was a huge sense of trepidation locally as it was so rare for a young boy to go missing. And more so for a teenage boy walking back to school on a busy road to disappear without a trace.

Nobody could state for sure that they had seen Philip that afternoon after he had left the family home. There was not one confirmed, unequivocal sighting of the boy, even though the road he would have walked down was extremely busy during that time. There were a few reports of people spotting boys fitting Philip's description that day but none that could categorically be stood up as definitely being him.

There is the very small probability that a motorist or someone walking in or out of their large semi-detached house on Ballyroan Road missed Philip being dragged into a car kicking and screaming. But if he had been pulled into a vehicle, he would have no doubt put up a fight and someone would have heard his cries for help and rushed to his aid.

There would also have been many teenagers returning to school at the time, yet none of them spotted him. Did any of them witness what happened that day but were too terrified to tell their parents or the authorities? So, the question is, did Philip willingly get into the car of someone he knew or recognised that day or was he snatched when nobody happened to be around to witness it?

Apart from the aforementioned Mary Boyle, which remains Ireland's longest unsolved missing child case, and that of Bernadette Connolly, there are very few cases you can compare to Philip's. Back in 1986, parental kidnapping accounted for a large number of missing children cases in Ireland. Philip's case was entirely different in that he literally vanished off the face of the earth while on his way back to school in broad daylight. There was no evidence left behind by Philip or his suspected abductor which detectives could follow up on.

Despite extensive media coverage during the early days of the investigation, officers had no clues to work off and were left aimlessly searching for answers which didn't exist. But the lack of evidence didn't stop officers from working tirelessly.

A team of 25 highly-skilled detectives combed the area around Rathfarnham looking for Philip, who was last seen wearing his Colaiste Eanna uniform which consisted of a dark grey V-neck school jumper, grey shirt and trousers, a grey jacket with black squares and black leather shoes. Officers spent every waking hour searching local woodlands, derelict sites, wastelands and open spaces. They also carried out extensive house-to-house searches. Heavy rain and winds, remnants of Hurricane Charley, only added to the task at hand. Local rivers were also dredged and county council workers were even called in to lift manhole covers so the sewers could be scoured. No stone was left unturned.

Officers thought they had made a breakthrough when forestry workers in Co Wicklow reported seeing young boys in a shack near a local wood, one of whom fitted the teenager's description. Gardaí turned their attention to the Ballinameesda area, four miles from Wicklow Town, following the tip-off. But the hut turned out to be empty and there was no sign of the youngsters.

As the extensive hunt failed to throw up any new leads, detectives started to worry that the boy had in fact been kidnapped.

Retired Detective Inspector Gerry O'Carroll, who worked on the case, said huge Garda resources, unlike any he had ever seen before, were put into the search. "It was one of the biggest manhunts in my career. We had people from every department, from forensics to the murder squad, involved. We had search teams that were very experienced. We sent out teams of 20 or more men and if they found resistance at a house or if the person was reluctant to let them in to search the house, the attic, the shed, we got a warrant. We didn't meet that much resistance, most people were very cooperative. We went through a hell of a lot of houses within about three miles of the epicentre of where he disappeared."

A roadblock was set up outside the Cairns' house during a busy lunchtime to try to establish just how hectic the Ballyroan Road was at roughly the time Philip went missing.

On a similar school day at 1.30pm, officers clocked a staggering 147 cars, 14 pedestrians and cyclists and five schoolboys. Their findings further enhanced just how busy the road was and how difficult a task it would have been for a stranger to abduct Philip without anyone noticing.

A number of cars including a blue Hiace van, an Orange Fiat 128 sports car, a beige vehicle and a red car were also all reported as acting suspiciously in and around the area at the time of Philip's disappearance.

There was one possible sighting of Philip which gardaí took very seriously at the time. A man on his way to the airport wrote down the registration number on a slip of paper of a red car, possibly a Mazda or Renault, which was badly parked and obstructing traffic on Ballyboden Road. Unfortunately, while away, his wife cleaned out his car and in the process threw the scrap of paper with the car's registration on it into the bin.

The local man said he saw a teenager, dressed in the Colaiste Eanna uniform, approaching the passenger side door of the car which was holding the traffic up. He described the person behind the wheel of the vehicle as a man who was around 50 years of age at the time and with grey sticky-up hair.

All frustrated detectives could do at the time was grit their teeth and thank the man for coming forward. It was reported at the time that officers, in a bid to retract any possible information surrounding the sighting of the car that day, even went so far as sending the man to a number of hypnosis sessions in both Ireland and England. It was hoped that they would allow him to recollect the registration number plate he had seen that day. But the man was unfortunately unable to recall any further details about the red car in question.

O'Carroll said it was the one sighting which he vividly remembered. "There was a guy who was going to the airport who identified a boy who looked like Philip Cairns walking towards a car. He took the number of the car but then went on holiday and when he came back it was gone. That always hung over the investigation. Was it Philip Cairns? Was it the person who abducted him?"

On Wednesday, October 29, teachers and pupils from his class at Colaiste Eanna were called back from their mid-term break to be interviewed by a team of 18 detectives for three hours in an effort to gather as much information as possible which might lead to the boy's whereabouts.

The students at the school, which was founded by the Christian Brothers in 1967, each had to give a statement. Officers described the series of interviews, which took place from 10am to 1pm, as "worthwhile" as they had thrown up names of other boys who knew Philip and played football with him and who might have had information surrounding his disappearance. All of the boys' classmates said they had not seen him since he left the school that afternoon to head home for lunch.

Detective Inspector Pascal Anders said at the time how they were getting great assistance from the public. "It is a job for everybody. It is everyone's concern when a child is missing. The police are depending on the public. People often think that what little they know is of no importance. But everyone who knows Philip, no matter how slightly, should talk to us. We'll decide what is important and what is not."

The young boy who sat beside Philip throughout primary and secondary school, Graham Callaghan, said the teenager was a lovely boy who he had great fun with. He recalled how nice his classmate was to be around. "We were in primary school together. We went to a special class together for English and he sat beside me. Then, when we went into secondary school at Colaiste Eanna, we sat beside each other too. He was very quiet but we had a laugh. He loved the camaraderie, sitting beside someone he could trust. He was a lovely lad who was never boisterous. He always did his homework and came in and would chat away to me."

Graham recalled the day his school pal disappeared and the devastating impact it had on all of the boys in his class. "He went out of that school gate and never returned. His demeanour was just the same as any other day. He went on break and just never came back. The library was turned into a response unit and we were all called back from our holiday to be interviewed. I remember sitting down and there was a detective and a councillor who said, 'You are not in trouble, I will speak for you and there is no need to feel any panic'. There were two to every table. I will never forget it."

He still thinks about Philip and what may have happened to him. He said the teen's disappearance has instilled a sense of fear in him right up until the present day when it comes to his own kids' safety. "I have three children, who are more or less grown up now, but I have spoken to them over the years and warned them to be safe when going out. It has stuck with me over the years. I tried to tell them that they were not bulletproof and there are people out there who might target them."

On Monday, November 3, all 573 students would return to the school. However, one seat would remain empty. There was still no trace of Philip. Following interviews with all of the students, gardaí confirmed they were investigating one line of enquiry which centred around claims that the teenager could have been the target of bullying by older boys at the school. There was talk amongst his fellow pupils that he may have been targeted simply for being religious. Detectives looked into this theory but it was later ruled out by officers and they were back to square one.

The following day, officers turned their attention to nearby Sancta Maria School and the Mercy Convent beside Philip's secondary. Pupils at the two schools travelled alongside Ballyroan Road and shared two shortcuts. Officers were hoping that interviewing the 850 or so girls from Sancta Maria would lead to some key witnesses coming forward, perhaps even the last person to see Philip alive. But yet again the detectives' efforts yielded no results.

At the family home, Philip's aunt said they were not giving up hope. "We are trying to think positively. Inevitably at this stage we fear the worst, but we refuse to abandon hope. His two sisters, Suzanne and Helen, returned to school but his younger brother Eoin was too upset to face it." Philip's disappearance had a massive impact on his school friends. A special mass was also organised at the Church of the Holy Spirit by school principal Brendan Vaughan "to give support to the Cairns family" who were deeply religious.

Mr Vaughan would say years later how everyone at the school joined together in a bid to try to find the boy. "I can remember we all went out and helped with the search, it was the neighbourly thing to do. Philip had just entered the secondary school the previous October, so I wouldn't have known him very well, but his younger brother, Eoin, went to the school as well and he was a fine young man. It was so sad to think of what his poor parents and indeed his whole family went through."

It was back on the evening of October 29, just hours after detectives interviewed students from the teenager's class, officers investigating the suspected abduction finally thought they had the breakthrough they had been hoping for.

Philip's faded grey schoolbag was found in a laneway at 7.45pm, half a mile from his family home.

Two 18-year-old girls, Orla O'Carroll and Catherine Hassett, found the battered and frayed bag while walking through the dark, 100-yard laneway which served as a shortcut for locals between Anne Devlin Road and Anne Devlin Drive. The bag had Philip's first name faintly scribbled on the front of it in black marker, lying next to a lamppost. One of them had passed through the laneway a few times earlier that day but said there was no sign of the bag then, which only lent further to the suggestion that it had only recently been placed there.

Following the discovery, the two teens ran straight to Rathfarnham Garda Station with the bag which was covered in U2 and UB40 black biro doodles. It was bone dry despite lashing rain on and off for most of the day.

A Garda spokesperson said at the time how the bag had "appeared quite mysteriously" and they were of the opinion that there may have been a sinister motive behind it. It was also suspected that the person who had the bag may have dropped it back under the cloak of darkness as they stood less chance of being noticed. After all, officers were still swarming the area and the person would have been more likely to be spotted during daylight hours. Regardless of the time, day or night, they were taking a massive risk dropping it back. Detectives were adamant it was not in the lane following Philip's disappearance as it had been thoroughly searched the days after the boy went missing.

Was it a coincidence that the satchel was found on the same day as detectives visited Philip's school to interview fellow students? Had the officers' presence at the all-boys secondary school that morning spooked someone?

It's also understood that someone close to the Cairns family asked detectives at the time of the discovery of the bag if it would be possible to have it checked against all the fingerprints from people at Philip's school. But the task was seen as far too demanding at the time. It would involve all of the students and those working at the school giving their samples voluntarily as they would have been under no obligation to give them. One idea behind the suggestion is believed to have been to rule out that an innocent student who stumbled across the bag had left it back in the laneway. If a local child was forced or coaxed by Philip's abductor to put the bag back, their prints may have been left on the bag also.

There is still a possibility that some of the fingerprints on Philip's bag and books will one day yield some answers. Officers are still hopeful that the person or people who dropped the satchel in the lane will one day come forward and finally solve one of the investigation's biggest mysteries. It's an aspect of the case which has played on the minds of Philip's family and officers investigating his disappearance since its discovery. The person who dropped it back could hold the key to potentially solving the case and bringing the pain Philip's family continues to suffer to an end.

When the bag was found officers also carried out an intensive search of a woodland area near the laneway.

The acre of undergrowth was behind a two-storey house which had fallen into disrepair and was often used by local teens for parties. Inspector Pat King said at the time that the books which were still in the bag were being examined by forensic experts and were being checked to see if any of the pages were missing.

Philip's mother, Alice, said he would have only used the laneway in question occasionally, when making his way to the library or church. As she was being comforted by her sister, Mary Brennan, who had travelled from Kilkenny, she told how she was praying that the discovery would help to find her son. "I am hoping for anything at all. We have no leads."

Did the person who abducted Philip leave the bag there or did a concerned member of the public, who did not wish to be drawn into the investigation, place it there after discovering it discarded in the area? The guards had only visited Philip's school that afternoon to question all of the students about his disappearance. Did the Garda presence at the school that day make a pupil who may have come across the satchel panic and decide to discard it? Did Philip's abductor leave it back or coax or threaten someone, perhaps a young child or teenager, to leave it there?

At the time, following the discovery of the bag, Superintendent Frank Hanlon appealed to whoever left it in the laneway to come forward. "We are very anxious to clear up the whole question of the bag and we want to talk to whoever left it there. They will be in no trouble, so we urge them to contact us."

# 3

## Hope and Heartache

*'Please, please, please help us and
you will be helping yourself ... I ask
you again, please come forward.
Call the police again. You do not need
to give your name'*

On Saturday, November 1, a mystery caller contacted the gardaí claiming to have seen a man carrying a schoolbag similar to the one Philip owned close to the area. The anonymous caller claimed the bag was being carried on the man's back. Despite them taking the call seriously, officers found it hard to believe that the person in question would not have at least tried to conceal the satchel if he was acting suspiciously.

Superintendent Hanlon said at the time how they wanted to talk to the anonymous man who was allegedly seen with the bag close to the laneway at the time. "We are very anxious to talk to that person. We would ask him for God's sake to come forward, we need to talk to him." The type of bag Philip was using as a schoolbag was extremely popular at the time, especially among teenagers his age.

A resident who lived close to the laneway, Bridie Fitzgerald, recalled the evening it was discovered. "It was found in the lane beside my back garden wall, I'll never forget it," she told the *Evening Herald* in 2015. "The story was already in the news and it was an awful sad event locally, and then I came home that evening and the gardaí and the locals were all outside and there was a big commotion. I was worried that whoever left it there had been in my garden. The gardaí searched my house and attic and everything, but nothing was ever found after that."

During the course of the search for Philip, diviners were called in to help try to find the boy. They were said to have been a great source of comfort to the Cairns family at the time of the disappearance.

One particular diviner even enthusiastically told Alice that, as far as he was concerned, her boy was still alive. Alice told the press at the time how she had given some of her son's belongings to him in an effort to  track the teenager. "We were asked for used rather than washed clothes and we gave him Philip's pyjamas and little shorts." The diviner – John Proud, from Dalkey, Co Dublin, who claimed to have a 90 per cent success rate, said at the time: "I think his discovery is imminent." But despite his enthusiasm, Philip's heartbroken mother was less optimistic and said she believed her son was being held against his will. "I still think he has been abducted and is being held somewhere."

After Philip's case made national headlines, a series of bogus telephone calls were made to the incident room. The hoax calls greatly hindered the guards' search and brought untold upset and pain to the Cairns family. Officers started to receive the sinister calls just days after the teen's disappearance and they would continue in the weeks and months that followed.

The weekend after Philip went missing, a company in Tallaght received a call from a teenager claiming to be the boy. It was recorded on an answering machine at the time and said: "I am Philip Cairns. I ran away from home. I can't go home. Tell my family I'm sorry. Thank you." However, gardaí were adamant that the voice was that of an older teenager, perhaps a 15 or 16-year-old and not Philip.

In the days following the teenager's disappearance, the Cairns family also received a series of "silent and sobbing phone calls". Not only had the family to contend with the pain of not knowing where their son and sibling was, they also had to endure these hurtful and malicious calls to their family home. In one incident, a twisted individual called the Cairns family and remained silent while a young boy could be heard crying in the background. The guards said at the time: "The disappearance is high profile with all the media coverage and there are people out there who make these types of calls in this situation."

Detective Sergeant Tom Doyle, who headed the investigation into Philip's disappearance between 1998 and 2016, said the family received many hoax calls over the years and were cruelly tormented by sick and twisted individuals claiming to know what had happened to the young teen. And he said no family, especially one going through so much unbearable pain, should have to endure such distress. "There was a lot of mistreatment of the family. There were people ringing and saying they knew where Philip was. They got a call from a member of the public at one stage to say he was in Swords Garda Station, that they had him and didn't want to discuss it too much over the phone, and asked them to head over.

"His poor father left work and they drove over and, sure, the guards in Swords had no idea what they were talking about as it had not been them who called. There were several occasions like that which they were exposed to. We call it trolling today but it was done differently back then. They suffered horrendous heartache at the time."

Despite extensive man hours being spent on the investigation, gardaí were still none the wiser as to what had happened to the teenager. They were unable to piece together any of his movements after he had walked out the front door of the family home on the afternoon of October 23. They decided to carry out a reconstruction of the boy's last known movements in a bid to jog people's memories.

On Tuesday, November 4, a volunteer Philip Cairns lookalike named Ultan Whelan set off on his "memory jogging" walk along Ballyroan Crescent. He was chosen to play the part of Philip by the schoolboy's best friend, 12-year-old Enda Cloke. Of similar height and build to the teenager, he was dressed in the same school uniform Philip was last seen wearing when he disappeared. Young Ultan confessed to being "a little nervous" as he retraced Philip's footsteps.

At the time, all the heartbroken Cairns family could do was watch on tearfully as their loved one's lookalike walked out of their home and retraced Philip's journey.

Alice said on the day how the person who took her son might have been worried about the repercussions if they came forward but pleaded with them to do the right thing and release Philip. "They must be in the situation where they feel they can't release him. They may feel nervous to let him go. But I will hold nothing against them. Revenge is not going to help." And she called on Philip's abductors to pray for strength in order to do the right thing. "The Lord will guide them. He in turn will protect them, he loves everybody." Following the reconstruction, which was shown on RTÉ's Evening Extra, gardaí received a large number of calls from the public offering information. Sadly, no details of value were received.

At the same time as the reconstruction, Superintendent Frank Hanlon was asked if there was any link between Philip's disappearance and that of his neighbour, John McGloughlin, who tragically went missing three years earlier in 1983. The 50-year-old failed to return home from work and was never found. But Supt Hanlon said there was no reason to believe the two cases were linked.

On Thursday, November 6, in a tragic case of coincidence, a 26-year-old man, Brendan Houlihan, who had been looking up Philip's baptismal certificate for a priest at St. Columba's church on Iona Road, Glasnevin, was brutally murdered. The body of the church sacristan was found partly clothed in the Royal Canal Dublin after his parents, Michael and Bridie, became concerned. He had locked up the church at 9pm and was on his way to deliver some church letters when he was savagely killed. Some of his clothes were missing and he was only partly dressed in just his vest, underpants and socks. Part of his shirt had also been ripped off and stuffed into his mouth and the letters he intended on delivering the night before were floating on the water close by. Headlines at the time included 'Hunt for canal bank killer of a gentle young man'.

Parish priest Tom Fehily said at the time, in an interview with the Irish press, how the whole parish was shocked at Mr Houlihan's shocking murder. And he recalled the events leading up to his death. "We spent yesterday afternoon looking up the church register to establish when little Philip Cairns was baptised here. His family lived in the area for some time." He said he had asked Mr Houlihan to check the records. Fr Fehily also said that the local congregation had been offering prayers in the church that the teenager would be found safe and well.

Two Dublin brothers were later charged and sentenced in connection to Mr Houlihan's death in October 1987. It was reported at the time that John Kenna, 24, of Dorset Street Flats, was jailed for 10 years after admitting the manslaughter of the young man. He was also given a concurrent four-year sentence for stealing his clothes and watch. His younger brother Declan Kenna, 17, from Cremona Road, Ballyfermot, was handed three years after pleading guilty to the robbery charge, newspapers at the time stated. Supt Patrick McGuinn, of Fitzgibbon Street Station, told the court that John Kenna had made a statement in which he had said: "He was roaring so much I put the shirt around his mouth. I gave him a few kicks and digs and he was struggling with me all the time."

On Monday, November 10, close to 300 local volunteers – including neighbours and friends of Philip – helped out in yet more searches for the youngster, combing woodlands and fields in the foothills of the Dublin Mountains. Among those helping in the search were experienced hill walkers who had come equipped with walking boots and sticks. Friends of Philip from the Dublin Sea Angling Club also joined in the search for the teenager.

Although a number of random items of clothing were found by volunteers throughout the day, gardaí ruled them out as being significant or connected to the case. Posters appealing for information of the missing teen were also circulated to every post office in the country. The local Association of Combined Residents printed off 2,096 posters featuring a picture of Philip, who at this stage was missing for 19 days and whose smiling face was known by pretty much every household in the country.

A number of reported sightings of the teen were made to gardaí in the days and weeks that followed. They included one in Carrick-on-Suir, Co Tipperary, which was later ruled out to be a boy who had missed his bus to Galway and had slept rough before hitching a lift.

There were also alleged sights of Philip in Dublin's north inner city, around Manor Street, the North Circular Road and Aughrim Street as well as at the McKee army barracks in Dublin and at a chalet in Tramore, Co Waterford. And they weren't just confined to Ireland, with the missing teen also being placed in Wales, London and mainland Europe. After a fortnight, Interpol also joined in the search for the missing boy. The decision was made by detectives to involve the European policing agency as their investigations in Ireland had drawn a blank. They were willing to try anything to try and track down the missing boy.

Philip's family were now certain that their eldest son had been snatched by some evil abductor. The schoolboy's father said at the time of his disappearance that he would have been smart enough not to have entered the vehicle of someone he didn't know. He was not foolhardy and would have known if someone unknown to him was trying to coax him into their car. "Certainly, he would never have got into a car with a stranger and if anybody had tried to force him, he would have put up a fight."

Did Philip know his abductor and therefore have no reason to believe he was in danger? Or was he coaxed into a car under false pretences by someone he simply could not say no to? Was there a child or teenager already in the car, perhaps even known to him, who put him at ease by their presence?

Detective Inspector Gerry O'Carroll, who was based at Sundrive Garda Station in Crumlin at the time of the disappearance, backed up this school of thought. He said that he would go so far as to say that he believed the person responsible for the teenager's abduction was probably someone known to the Cairns family or someone who was deemed as a pillar of society. And he said that's why it is likely nobody heard Philip scream or witnessed a struggle, because the boy willingly got into their car unaware of the danger which lay ahead.

"I was always convinced that he was picked up by somebody who he knew. He got into a car with someone he knew and trusted. The person knew about his routine, about him going home for lunch, what time he would leave to head back to school. I asked myself, 'How could a young boy disappear off a busy road in Ireland at 1.30pm in the day?' We were hoping we would make a breakthrough with some motorist saying, 'I saw the little fella with his schoolbag,' but no, never, not one sighting. I mean, if a child is abducted, there's a struggle, something. It's very hard to do something, no matter what it is or how secretive you are, without someone observing it, even from a distance."

O'Carroll believes it's highly likely that the person who abducted Philip that day was one of the 1,600 locals who were interviewed during the initial course of the investigation.

After a month of being away from home, his mother Alice said she was struggling to get her head around when and how exactly he might have been taken. She said the window of time was so short between him leaving the family home and disappearing. "It's only a 10-minute walk to school and there are houses all along the way. It's hard to figure out what might have happened to him between here and the school, unless someone is holding him. But all the areas have been searched. Please God, he'll come back the way he went – as quietly and as healthy."

The hunt for Philip over the years never stopped nor diminished. O'Carroll said many officers, even those who were no longer working on the case, held a torch for the missing boy. The former officer said he even carried out unofficial searches and digs with colleagues himself years later after receiving information from various informants.

"When I was at Sundrive Road years later, I was given a few locations where his body was supposedly buried and one of them was up near Woodtown. I remember going in there and searching. We did a very detailed search. I didn't want to be spooking the authorities or causing a ruckus, I did it with a couple of colleagues of mine from Sundrive Road. We dug ourselves but we never found anything.

"Another location was given to us and, when we got there, there was a big factory built on it, so that was the end of that. The information wasn't that solid. People knew I was involved in the Philip Cairns case and would ring me and say, 'I know where his body is'. But I just couldn't ignore it."

Chief Superintendent Michael McKeon, who was in charge of the investigation at the time, updated the public and media on the case during a press conference and said officers were still baffled as to what had happened to the young boy. And he said at that stage they were of the belief he was still alive as there was no proof to state otherwise. "We are keeping a very open mind on it. We have no evidence to show or any reason to believe he is dead. But we are mindful that he is now missing since the 23rd of October without a trace."

Philip's heartbroken father felt differently, however, but said at the time that the family would maintain hope that he was still out there. "After eight weeks of not knowing what has happened, the uncertainty makes life very, very difficult. I'm still hoping, but I'm very worried at this point. I have to keep hoping, otherwise I just couldn't carry on."

Philip's mother also made an anguished pre-Christmas plea for his safety at an emotional press conference on December 16. "If anyone has abducted my son, please soften your hearts and think of us. Please bring our nightmare to an end. I am still hoping, but I am very, very worried." Philip Snr added: "If anybody is holding Philip I would appeal to them in the season of goodwill that they would let him go, or contact someone and let us know he is safe."

Philip was in good spirits before he went missing and was even looking forward to Christmas, despite it being a few months away. He was excited about the prospect of getting new fishing equipment and had mentioned it to his mother one day in passing. His happy demeanour and plans for the festive season certainly did not match those of someone who was planning on running away.

On Christmas Eve, 1986, his heartbroken mother recalled the earlier conversation the pair had about Christmas and gifts. "I remember when I raised the subject I thought he might ask for a bike because I knew that's what he'd love. He is not the type of child who expects the earth."

On February 21, 1987, four months after the Rathfarnham youth vanished, friends and neighbours held a 12-hour vigil at the local Church of the Holy Spirit. Mr and Mrs Cairns attended the special mass where they were joined by hundreds of locals. There wasn't a single person within the community who didn't feel for the family and the whole neighbourhood rallied around them to offer their support. Parish Priest, Fr Christopher Kenny, paid tribute to the Cairns family's faith during the terrible time of crisis. "It is an inspiration to us all – we have learned a lot from Philip's family," he told the packed congregation.

Philip's younger brother Eoin served as one of the altar boys at the service, which had been organised by local youngsters. They included some drawn from the scouts, the Ray folk group of young pioneers and pupils from Philip's school as well as the all-girls Catholic secondary school, Sancta Maria, which was originally established by the Mercy Sisters and which two of his sisters attended. Alice expressed her gratitude to the young people of the parish who had organised the event, which ran from midday to midnight.

In a heartfelt speech to those in attendance, she said: "We still have not given up hope that he will come back. We wait every day for the news that he is coming home. The family is coping well. We have got great support from all sections of the parish."

The case was never far from the news headlines and, in April 1987, it was reported that an alleged sex offender had sought refuge at Kevin Street Garda Station after an angry mob of about 70 people broke up his flat in Dublin city centre when it was reported in a national newspaper that he was believed to be a child abuser. Officers investigating Philip's disappearance were called in to interview the man from Fatima Mansions, Rialto, but they ruled out any connection to the teenager's case, the *Evening Herald* reported at the time.

The months quickly turned into years and every October Philip's devastated family would make heartfelt appeals on TV and in the national press for their missing loved one, pleading to anyone with information about his whereabouts to come forward. But no credible new leads ever emerged and all the Cairns family could do was hope and pray that someone with vital information would come forward.

In 1989, three years after her son disappeared, Alice said despite the struggle to keep going, she had tried to remain positive. "It's hard to wonder where he might be for three years but you have to keep hoping that he will be back." Philip Snr was also continuing to question what exactly had happened to his son on that dreaded day. "It is such a busy road around lunch time you would wonder if it would be possible to drag him into a car without someone noticing the incident. Then how did the schoolbag turn up? If he went voluntarily they wouldn't fling the schoolbag away. They would take the bag with them. No matter which way you look at it, it doesn't come right."

But what if Philip never made it far along the busy Ballyroan Road, what if he was abducted just metres away from his front gate? As one detective told me, there is a high probability nobody saw him getting into a car that day because it happened just moments after he left his family home. Former Detective Inspector O'Carroll said: "I believe he (the abductor) may have waited close to the house and pulled onto the hard shoulder. You can't just park at the side of that road. They pulled in somewhere extremely close by, I'm talking not 10 feet away."

O'Carroll believes the person behind his kidnapping would have struggled to keep Philip quiet or hide him away. "I think he was killed that day. Was it to shut him up? Now this is the big thing. You take somebody to silence somebody. You kill someone who's going to shop you and get you 10 or 15 years in prison. Put it this way, it wasn't a normal abduction."

He dismisses the theory that it could have been a random paedophile on the prowl who took him. "They would have taken a child in town or somewhere else, not from outside his house. Did he know something? Did the killer suspect he was going to report him to the gardaí? Was this person a pillar of the community? I have no doubt he was taken by a pillar of the community. You can't discount anybody."

Philip's aunt Terry Moore was also of the belief that it could have been someone close to the Cairns family. When talking on the Gay Byrne programme in 1986 she said she believed the abductor was known to her nephew and the family. "It has to be a neighbour or somebody well-known to the family. I don't think he would have got into the car with anyone unless there was a special reason that was plausible to him."

Officers started to narrow down the number of potential suspects to a "small select few". Detectives also believed the person behind the kidnapping also had an extensive knowledge of the Ballyroan area, which would only be known to a resident, someone who had once lived there or an individual who frequented the area.

There were many twists and turns in the investigation. In late 1989, four anonymous calls to the investigation team raised their hopes once again. The information received within the conversations now pointed officers towards a new line of enquiry. Gardaí arranged to meet with the unnamed caller who came forward with substantial information but unfortunately the person responsible never turned up. Detectives believed that the details supplied to them by this unidentified individual were completely authentic and would have only been known to somebody with inside knowledge of the case. At the time they also appealed to a Dublin woman who contacted them in relation to the investigation and who said she had information about the disappearance but had difficulty in passing it on.

Superintendent Bill McMunn, leading the investigation, said at the time: "Recently, we have received a number of telephone calls from an unidentified source. These calls contained specific information. We are treating those calls extremely seriously and in order to evaluate the information we are very anxious that this person should again contact us. We can assure this person or any other caller that this information will be treated in the strictest confidence. In the end we hope that this might give us the break we are hoping for." Anyone with information at the time was asked to call the Garda confidential telephone number on 599554.

Philip's father appealed to those who had made earlier contact with the gardaí to get back in touch. "The tension and stress is there all the time, you can't relax. You can't really enjoy anything or give anything full concentration, it's just the one thing on your mind. You have to try and suppress it, try and put it out of your mind. I beg anyone who has the slightest bit of information to come forward, even at this late stage."

In November 1989, Philip's aunt Terry wrote an open letter pleading to the man who had rang the Garda station on a number of occasions to get back in touch. She described the heartbreak the family were going through not knowing what had happened to Philip and begged the caller to come forward and help end their suffering.

She wrote: "On behalf of my nephew, Philip Cairns, and his family, I am making this appeal. I am appealing to the man who rang the police station on several occasions and gave information that they took very seriously, the man who arranged to go to the station on several occasions, but never turned up. I would like to let this man know I am sorry for his dilemma. After all, for all we know, it could be his neighbour, or even friend or friends. He must have been hoping the police would solve the case without him, but now he knows this is unlikely and he, God help him, is struggling with his conscience and saying, 'I'll wait another day, they may not need me'. Well, the police do need him badly."

The impact of Philip's disappearance on her brother, Philip Snr, Alice and the teenager's siblings had been immense. "The agony my brother and his wife, and in fact on all of us in not knowing what happened, is past comprehension. Unless you have to live through it as we are living, day and night, week after week, year after year. And it never gets any better. It is like a horror story with no end, but it is not fiction and therefore more horrendous. But I would like to point out to this man that the terrible state of our minds will be nothing to the state of his, if, in not helping the police now, another child vanishes into the blue like Philip.

"The fact that this has not happened so far does not mean it will not happen today, tomorrow, or even in a year's time. I do not think this man had a hand, act or part in Philip's disappearance, but if he does not help now, he will certainly be responsible if the same person or persons do it again. He will not be able to live with himself and God only knows, I would not wish this on my worst enemy. Although worried and afraid, he should not be afraid. If he brings peace of mind to Philip's family he can only be doing a very good and charitable act. He will also be helping the person responsible for the crime."

Philip's devastated aunt concluded: "Please, please, please help us and you will be helping yourself. Dear sir, in desperation, I ask you again, please come forward. Call the police again. You need not give your name, just answer some questions and that is all. So do ring and help all concerned."

Investigating officers and Philip's family pleaded with the man in question to come forward, again to no avail. Superintendent Bill McMunn said years later that he believed the calls may have been a hoax.

The family, already having to contend with the grief of not knowing what had happened to their little boy, now had to come to terms with the fact that they had to rely on members of the public to cooperate with authorities. They also had to face the realisation that there were many twisted individuals out there who just wanted to add to their already unbearable suffering and grief with hoax calls and information.

During the same month, gardaí also searched a misused dump in the Dublin Mountain foothills known as Woodlawn Quarry on Stocking Lane in Rathfarnham.

Detectives decided to focus their energy on the area after a resident came forward claiming to have witnessed two men acting suspiciously in the days following Philip's disappearance. They claimed to have seen the men at 2am on Wednesday, November 5, less than two weeks after the teen had been reported missing, taking a large black plastic bag from the boot of their vehicle which they then set on fire.

At the time the resident told the *Sunday World*: "The fire burned for most of the night and I became suspicious and decided to call the gardaí. I knew it was a long shot but I thought it best that they be told of everything." Unfortunately, the dig amounted to nothing and detectives were back to square one.

# 4.

# Missing

*'It's the whole deep question mark of it. What happened? Was it something I did? And that's all part of the process. People blame themselves'*

On average, one person is reported missing in Ireland every hour of every day. Despite the high number, the vast majority return home within days, safe and well.

Sadly, some of those who disappear include the tragic cases of those who have taken their own life. Then there are incidents where people who have been reported missing actually want to walk away from the life they are living and start over, unfortunately leaving concerned loved ones in the dark as to their whereabouts. It is very rare therefore, and there are generally only a small handful of cases each year, where people simply vanish without a trace never to be seen again and there is no plausible explanation behind it.

The vast majority of missing persons cases reported to gardaí are of adults, which is classed as anyone over the age of 18. When it comes to missing children, a high number of juveniles who are reported to authorities have either disappeared of their own accord, run away from home, or are cases of parental abduction. A missing person is deemed, 'Anyone whose whereabouts are unknown and the circumstances of the disappearance presents a risk of harm to the missing person or any other person,' according to the Garda website.

The case of Philip Cairns is still being treated as a missing person case in spite of many, including detectives who have worked on the case, believing it should be upgraded to a murder investigation. According to one detective I spoke to, the investigation should be one of murder as it's most likely he is no longer alive and that he may have met a sinister end. The former officer pointed out that it is hard to change the status of the case without any remains being discovered. But he did also suggest that in other jurisdictions it has been done.

In Ireland, The Missing Persons Unit falls under the remit of the Garda National Protective Services Bureau (GNPSB) and is currently overseen by Superintendent Gerard Murphy. The unit provides advice, guidance and assistance to gardaí who are investigating missing person incidents. It also helps when human remains are discovered and can't be identified.

Latest Garda figures for missing people cases showed there were 8,485 incidents reported in 2020. Up until October of that year alone, 52 had still not been traced, including 18 children. In total, 823 cases remain open with the longest dating back as far as 1951. According to Sergeant Carmel Griffin of the Garda Missing Persons Bureau, the files of missing persons are reviewed on a regular basis regardless of how much time has passed since initially being reported to them. She said that scientific breakthroughs in DNA tracking and the establishment of the National Missing Persons database in 2015, which is managed by Forensic Science Ireland (FSI), had played a huge role in helping to close some of the longest-running unsolved cases.

Speaking in 2020, Sgt Griffin said it was important for families of those missing to give DNA samples which can then be uploaded onto their database. "A missing persons case remains open until they are found. We never give up looking for them. We never forget about them. There is a constant series of reviews of cases, right back to the longest-running case. I'd like people to realise that we really do never give up. We never close a missing persons investigation until the person is found. We need the help of the public because sometimes it might be a small piece of information that they might think is inconsequential that might be of assistance in providing a new direction. People should never be afraid to come forward."

Sgt Griffin said there were cases where people deliberately disappeared too but, even in those instances, they would ask the person to get in touch so that they could let their concerned family know they were safe and well.

"There is no certain demographic that is more prolific than any other. It's people's current situation. The other side to all this is that some people have lost contact with their families and they may have been reported missing. I would like them to know they can contact the gardaí and let them know they are safe and their location will not be shared with their family, there is no judgement. Sometimes people go missing for whatever reason and they don't feel that they can return, or contact their families anymore. Some people just want to disappear. We urge people in that position to get in touch with us, if anything just so we can let their loved ones know they are safe. Maybe they want to make sure their family knows they are safe without them having to talk to them directly, and we are happy to provide that service. Every case is so unique and so different and it is only when you dig down and investigate that you find that, in certain circumstances, it is the case that someone does not want to be found."

There have also been a number of cases solved thanks to advancements in new DNA technology.

They included the cases of 18-year-old James Gallagher, from Cabra in Dublin, who disappeared in 1999; 49-year-old Margaret Glennon, from Baldoyle in North Dublin, who was reported missing in 1995, and Conor Whooley, who disappeared in 1983.

Mr Whooley, from Greystones in Co Wicklow, was successfully identified after his family provided DNA which was tested against remains which had been buried in Wales as part of the Garda's Operation Runabay. The operation was set up in 2017 to help identify the bodies of people who may have entered the Irish Sea and could have ended up on the west coast of Britain. Up until December 2019, it had helped to identify 10 missing people through family DNA samples

"Regardless of the background to these deaths, you have to remember there are families constantly waiting for some form of closure," Sgt Griffin said. "A very common emotion expressed is a desire for closure. They all want a grave to grieve. The big issue is the unknown, not knowing what happened to them," she told the *Irish Examiner*.

There are many high-profile cases which receive a lot of media coverage each year, including the missing women who disappeared in the mid to late 1990s around the Leinster area: Annie McCarrick, Deirdre Jacob, Eva Brennan, JoJo Dullard, Ciara Breen, Fiona Sinnott and Fiona Pender.

Rapist Larry Murphy, who was jailed after abducting, raping and almost murdering a Carlow businesswoman, is understood to remain a person of interest to gardaí for some of the unsolved cases. While jailed, the Wicklow carpenter emerged as a possible suspect for involvement in the disappearance of three of the women who vanished. He was allegedly quizzed by officers probing the cases of the missing women who are presumed dead, as part of Operation Trace. Murphy's method of kidnapping, raping and the attempted murder of the Carlow woman suggested to gardaí he was a seasoned predator.

Then there is the tragic case of 22-year-old Trevor Deely, who was reported missing on December 8, 2000, following a Christmas party in Dublin city centre. His heartbroken family have continuously kept his story in the media in the hope that one day they might find out what happened to him. Due to the high number of missing persons cases there are sadly many the public never gets to hear about, each with a devastated family at its core.

For a country with such high numbers of missing persons cases each year, close to 9,000, it's vital that the families get the support they need. One organisation which has proved invaluable to the loved ones of those who have disappeared is The National Missing Persons Helpline, a non-profit group founded by Dermot Browne in 2003. Mr Browne, who is chairperson of the charity which was set up following a family tragedy, said the service provides support and resources to anyone who needs it. The organisation also collects missing person case figures through public appeals made by the gardaí.

Mr Browne said: "There would be more than 9,000 reports every year to the gardaí. From our statistics there are only between 200 and 300 publicised so it's only a tiny percentage of missing person cases that people actually hear about.

"While we would keep statistics, they would only be on published cases because not all families would use our service, so therefore we wouldn't know of them. There would be organisations like our one in various countries around the world and each one operates differently with the resources that they have.

"We have a good relationship with the gardaí and it's something that we guard because it's obviously essential to the work we do. We provide whatever service we can within the means that we have to the families that contact us for support. I set up the organisation in 2003 and it started off as a loose affiliation of people who had an interest in it and were prepared to basically be at the end of the phone for anyone who wanted to talk. It's a small group of people who are involved, we get by on scraps and in my opinion are doing an essential service for people."

The charity offers advice to loved ones of those who have disappeared and tend to work on cases which have remained open and unsolved for a long time, Mr Browne said. "The area that we work in is the long-term missing persons because generally they are the ones who need the most support. They would generally contact us for information or advice on what to do and obviously the first thing that you do is tell them to contact the gardaí. The support would kick in when it becomes apparent that it may turn into a long-term case because while there is an initial interest in some of these cases, after a while they begin to fade into the background and the families do feel that they are left on their own to deal with it. It's up to people like ourselves to offer support and to keep it going on our Facebook page and website."

Mr Browne, whose tireless work has helped hundreds of heartbroken families over the years, believes that in most cases someone holds the vital information necessary to help trace a missing loved one.

"I'm very much of the belief that in every case somebody knows. They may not know that they know but they do. In some cases where some harm has come to a person, not by themselves, then somebody definitely does know. Even in cases where a person may have harmed themself there is always something that they would have said or done that people would be aware of but may not have taken note of that will help in the case and in finding them.

"It's amazing how a small piece of information can be the part that fits the jigsaw and brings it to completion. We are constantly trying to point out to people that the smallest piece of information can make the difference. It can bring meaning to other things that are there, that are just pieces of information, which when put together puts them all into perspective. The relief that a family gets once they are found is huge."

He added there has always been great public support when it

comes to the organisation but that a lot of people are shocked when they discover the extent of unsolved missing people cases here in Ireland.

"I know that when we put up our stand in shopping centres, people who come over to see us are amazed by the number of posters. They will be able to remember three or four high-profile cases, Philip Cairns being one and Mary Boyle another. But when they stand back and see all of the other people that nobody knows about, I do see women walking away from the stand in tears because they are so sad over the whole thing. Sadly, for families of those missing, they are left with feelings of unbearable guilt and many unanswered questions. It's the whole deep question mark of it. *What happened? Was it something I did?* And that's all part of the process. People blame themselves."

When it comes to missing children, many European countries, including Italy and Greece, have an alert system in place. Police forces across the UK, including the PSNI, have been operating a similar system called Child Rescue Alert since 2003. It was brought into the Republic of Ireland on May 25, 2012. Since then gardaí have been able to issue a Child Rescue Ireland Alert (CRI) if a juvenile has been taken and it is deemed that there is an immediate and serious risk to his or her welfare.

The system is an adaptation of the Amber Alert which first began in America in 1996, when broadcasters teamed up with local police authorities to develop a system which allowed for photos and information about a missing child to be circulated quickly.

It got its name from the tragic case of nine-year-old Amber

Hagerman, who was kidnapped and murdered while riding her bike in Arlington, Texas.

To date in Ireland it has proved extremely successful and has helped authorities to track down a number of children who were deemed to be in danger.

Over the years, advancements in DNA technology and systems like the Child Rescue Ireland Alert (CRI) have proved highly beneficial in missing person cases. The public is made aware of CRI alerts through social media and online newspaper websites.

Unfortunately, back in 1986 when Philip Cairns went missing, no hi-tech systems like this existed. Officers investigating his case had to rely on posters of the teenager being circulated and placed in shop windows and on the sides of milk bottles, a process which took days not minutes like with today's technology. However, advancements in technology – including DNA testing – could still prove crucial in finding out what happened to the teenage boy all those years ago.

It could also help officers, who continue to tirelessly investigate the other unsolved missing person cases, to get closure for some of the families who are silently waiting in hope for some answers as to where their loved one is.

# 5.

# Evidence

*'When they found the schoolbag,
we were all so relieved. We were
convinced that he was on his way
home and that he would be here within
a matter of minutes'*

The most significant development and the only evidence to ever be retrieved in the case was Philip's grey fabric schoolbag. From the day the teenager disappeared to the present day, no other item belonging to the teen has ever been found. Its discovery came six days after he was reported missing by his worried parents. Teenage friends Catherine Hassett and Orla O'Carroll were en route to their friend Amy's house at the time. But there was something about the canvas bag just sitting there which Catherine just couldn't ignore. Her curiosity got the better of her, so she decided the pair should inspect it closer.

Speaking for the first time in 35 years, she recalled to me how the two friends were initially terrified after they made the shocking discovery as they feared that the person who had left the bag in the laneway was still lurking close by. Locals were terrified and the neighbourhood children had been warned by their parents to be extra vigilant.

Catherine said it was dark and cold and there was a very eerie feeling in the air following Philip's disappearance. She said what the pair initially found strange about the bag upon its discovery was that it was bone dry, despite heavy rain showers earlier that day. Her friend Orla had also passed through the busy laneway a number of times earlier that afternoon and had not spotted it, leading them both to believe it had only recently been placed there. The laneway itself was used a lot by locals as a shortcut, too, and the bag would have easily been spotted prior to them stumbling upon it had it been there for some time. It was also placed in an area of the lane, beside a lamppost, which made it impossible to miss. It was clearly placed under the light so it would be easily seen.

Catherine recounted the scene: "Orla had been over and back through the laneway that day. Our friend, Amy, lived over in Orchardton and she had been over to see her. Orla lived in Ballyroan and I lived in Palmer Park. So I went down on my bike to Orla and we were heading through the lane.

"I was wheeling my bike and Orla was walking beside me. We were walking through the lane and the bag was on the ground as you came around the bend. I don't know what jogged it but I said, 'That's very strange to have a bag sitting there'. As we went to walk past it, I said, 'Orla, pick that up and just make sure it does not belong to that young fella who has gone missing'. Orla picked it up and said, 'No, no it belongs to someone beginning with C,' and I went, 'No, they spell Cairns with a C'."

She added: "It was very much just sitting there. It wasn't covered with any leaves or anything. Orla took out a copybook and showed it to me and when we realised it was his we went, 'Oh crap, do we go out the lane or do we go back the way we came?' It was like, 'Oh, dear Jesus'.

"We were scared in the lane, we wanted to get out of there because we were like, 'Ok, how can the bag be here?' Our first thought was to just get out. It was eerie, it just didn't fit. Philip had gone missing and he was missing nearly a week and then all of a sudden this bag was there. It just didn't make any sense."

Upon finding the bag, Catherine said the pair decided to race to the local Garda Station in Rathfarnham to hand the key piece of evidence over to officers investigating the case.

Orla jumped on to the back of her friend's bicycle and Catherine cycled as fast as her legs would allow. "As we made our way there, on the back of Marian Road, we came across a friend of ours, Cormac. He was in the garden standing at his dad's car so we told him what we had found and I threw my bike in the back of his house and he drove us down to the police station.

"We went down to Rathfarnham Garda Station and a detective came down and took the bag from us. We spoke to the detectives and they brought us back to the laneway. We showed them exactly where we had found the bag and where we had picked it up. Then they closed the lane off."

Gardaí informed Philip's parents of the sinister new lead

within an hour of the bag's discovery. The teenager's mother was confident and her hopes were raised upon hearing the news that suggested her boy might now possibly be found safe and well. "We are very hopeful that something might come of this, all we can do is keep praying," she said at the time.

Yet rather than the new evidence answering questions about her son's whereabouts, the bag being left in the lane ultimately only added to the confusion for her family and the investigation team. "The schoolbag is just one more mystery. It must have been planted. It couldn't have been lying there for all that time. It's hard to remain rational about this. You feel yourself slowly disintegrating," Alice said. Following the bag's discovery, she revealed that she initially expected the case to be solved and for her son to walk through the front door. "When they found the schoolbag, we were all so relieved. We were convinced that he was on his way home and would be here within a matter of minutes, so we all went out looking for him."

Catherine said all the clues pointed to the fact that the bag had only recently been left in the narrow lane and officers investigating the case said they were of the same belief, confirming that an extensive search of the area had been conducted after Philip was reported missing and nothing whatsoever had been found. "The police said they searched the laneway several times and Orla said she had gone through it throughout that day and had seen nothing. She went over to Amy's and back that day and never recalled seeing it at all. Our feeling was that it had just been placed there. We saw nobody around. We were halfway down the lane and came back on ourselves. We didn't see anybody ahead of us either."

Detective Garda John Harrington, now retired, was upstairs

in his office when the two girls arrived at the front desk of the Garda station with the bag.

Recalling the evening in question, he told me: "I was doing the paperwork on the case at the time. It was very rare for a child to be abducted off the side of the road. It would have been a huge case country-wide but particularly in the Tallaght and Rathfarnham area. I was up in the office when someone downstairs rang up and said two girls were after coming in with a schoolbag. I went down and took it off them and handed it over to the exhibits officer at the time."

Upon searching the bag, officers quickly discovered two of the boy's religion books were missing, the Good News New Testament Bible and the Christian Way Book 1. The missing bible also bore the name of Philip's school friend Shane Sweeney, who the book had been bought from. His geography book was also nowhere to be found.

All that remained was Philip's school journal, his copybook and a maths book. Were his religious books removed on purpose? It was believed to be the case at the time but was really pure speculation, fuelled by the fact that Philip and his family were religious, something that was not unusual in Ireland during the 1980s. Many families often attended mass on a Sunday. Looking back at many media reports at the time, there was very little mention of the fact that Philip's geography book was also missing from his bag, which only fed into the crazy theory that the schoolboy had been taken by a religious sect.

Catherine said her DNA was never taken, nor was her friend Orla's, to cross-reference against the samples on the bag. Despite DNA testing not existing in 1986, Catherine said she was surprised that they had not been approached since to offer samples which could be compared to those on the schoolbag. The bag is understood to have been scientifically tested in November 1987 but at the time did not reveal anything of value.

Catherine said many people, including investigating officers, handled the bag that evening alone. "What DNA testing did they carry out on the bag? Nobody ever took my DNA or Orla's. Nobody thought about it at the time. In fact, after we found it, I think they brought it back up to the laneway and they carried it and were not wearing gloves."

At the time, the use of DNA as evidence was unheard of and it would be years before it would be used in a criminal case in Ireland. Investigating officers working on the case have never publicly stated how many DNA samples are on the bag but it is believed that there are no singular profiles. Instead, there are a number of mixed DNA samples, making them extremely difficult – and in some scientists' eyes, impossible – to retrieve.

There were newspaper reports in recent years claiming that there were three separate DNA profiles lifted from the bag but this has never been officially confirmed by authorities and, according to one former officer I spoke to, is not believed to be the case.

If any singular profiles were discovered on the bag, they would have been compared against those which are currently stored on the DNA database by Forensic Science Ireland at the Garda Headquarters in the Phoenix Park. One detective told me: "As far as I am aware there are no clear single samples of DNA on the bag but loads of mixed DNA."

There is a high probability that Philip's abductor or the person or people who dropped the bag in the laneway unwittingly left their DNA on it. Whether it was the perpetrators or an innocent bystander who happened to stumble across it, their DNA is most likely within the mixed samples on the bag. There's also the possibility that vulnerable teenagers or children, known to Philip's kidnapper, dropped it back not realising its significance at the time. Or perhaps, as one officer pointed out, were made to do so under duress.

When it comes to a criminal investigation, DNA now plays a pivotal role in helping to solve many cases. Forensic Science Ireland (FSI) oversees the DNA testing of evidence in Irish criminal cases and has in the past examined the teenager's schoolbag. It wasn't until 1994 that FSI in Dublin introduced DNA technology into casework. The first time it was used in an Irish court was in the DPP V Mark Lawlor case. The suspect was accused of a sexual assault on an elderly woman, Rose Farrelly, who he murdered during a burglary at her home. DNA from semen found on the victim's clothing matched a profile which had been generated from his blood. The killer was handed a life sentence for the murder as well as nine years for burglary and an additional five years for the sexual assault.

In 2003, the Irish Attorney General requested the Law Reform Commission to consider the establishment of a National DNA Database, which was later introduced in 2014. Today, the DNA Database System is maintained and operated by FSI and helps to match DNA profiles from those under investigation, former offenders, convicted criminals and those which have been retrieved at a crime scene. Latest figures show that as of 2019, there were 27,565 profiles on the DNA database reference index.

So what exactly is DNA?

According to the FSI, the human body is composed of billions of cells of many different types, blood, skin, and bone to name but a few. Almost all cells contain a nucleus and within the nucleus of each cell is an identical copy of a person's DNA. Due to this DNA a person's blood will be the same as that found in their saliva or hair roots. As each person's DNA is inherited equally from their father and mother, everyone's is unique (except identical twins). The polymerase chain reaction (PCR) enables scientists to rapidly multiply small areas of DNA.

The first case in which DNA testing was used worldwide by investigators to determine the identity of a suspect was in 1987 in the UK, to help solve the 'Black Pad' killings. Double killer Colin Pitchfork was jailed over the rapes and murders of 15-year-olds Dawn Ashworth and Lynda Mann after becoming the first murderer to be snared using DNA evidence.

Following Dawn's murder in 1986, Leicestershire Police carried out the biggest manhunt in its history, calling on a staggering 5,000 local men to volunteer a sample of their saliva or blood as part of their investigation.

Pitchfork hatched a plan to evade capture by convincing a work colleague named Ian Kelly to take the test for him. But his masterplan backfired when Mr Kelly told friends at the pub what he had been asked to do and a witness to the conversation reported it to the police, who then arrested Pitchfork a short time later.

The FSI, which was established in 1975 to provide a scientific service to the Criminal Justice System by analysing samples, is made up of highly trained scientists and analysts. On occasion, scientists from FSI also attend crime scenes with members of the Crime Scene Investigation (CSI) team from the Garda Technical Bureau to offer their assistance.

According to FSI, even though each person's DNA is unique, with current technology it is not practical to look at each difference. It states that: "Currently in the laboratory we look at 16 different areas of DNA, which are known to have a wide variance within the Irish population. We also examine the gender indicator. The 16 areas contain short repeating sequences known as Short Tandem Repeats (STR). The number of these repeating sequences varies between individuals. The technique of DNA profiling is centred on analysing and measuring the differences in length of these STRs. An additional two peaks on the profile determines whether the person is male or female."

According to one former officer I spoke to, Irish scientists have not yet managed to pull profiles from the mixed DNA samples on the satchel.

One of the world's top DNA experts, Dr Mark Perlin, told me that many law enforcement agencies around the world do not yet have the technology necessary to carry out such tests. But Dr Perlin said he had devised a system which can in fact pull single profiles from mixed DNA, and in even the most complex cases, can return results in just a matter of days. And the doctor, who is renowned in the scientific world for developing a computer based statistical system, True Allele, which analyses forensic samples containing the DNA of two or more people, said his technology could be used to retrieve single profiles from the mixed samples on Philip's schoolbag.

The American doctor's method of analysing genetic samples has been used in hundreds of cases and in helping to identify the charred remains of victims of the 9/11 attack on the World Trade Center. Dr Perlin said when Philip disappeared in 1986, DNA testing was unheard of and instead investigators relied on far simpler methods, like fingerprints for example, as evidence. But he said nowadays DNA testing played a massive role in modern-day criminal investigations and could in many incidents help to solve a case.

"Nobody would have been thinking about DNA contamination in 1986 when Philip disappeared because it wouldn't become a thing for another 15 years. DNA is often the only evidence in a case. DNA evidence has the ability to tell an investigator when someone left their DNA when they weren't supposed to, that somebody was there when they weren't supposed to be, and that's the most powerful role of it. It also analyses the crime scene and interprets who was or wasn't present on different items of evidence. It can also map out a crime scene. There are some cases where the DNA just opens up the whole case. There are times when the DNA just tells you what happened."

The world-renowned specialist, whose technique is used in the New York police's forensic labs, said retrieving mixed DNA from an object was very complex. "We were the first to do it. I invented this about 20 years ago and it took many years to perfect the software. We have used it in about 1,000 cases and there are about 10 crime labs in the US who use it in their regular case work. We have used it in Northern Ireland too. I was involved in the Massereene Barracks case. There was a matchstick that was found at the side of a burnt-out car which was believed to have been used in the attack on the barracks. When they amplified the DNA in the lab they amplified it three times. And from each amplification there was so little DNA that they got a different signal, they had different data. But when our computer looked at all three of the data amplifications together it was able to pull out the DNA.

"Most of the time you don't have to amplify it so many times. This was extreme because the matchstick was burnt. When we worked on the World Trade Center project we had about 100,000 tests across 18,000 items but these were mainly charred victims' remains, and so by having multiple tests on the same item the computer could do more with the data."

The DNA expert explained how normal samples are tested, including in many of the forensic crime laboratories around the world. "The goal is to extract the DNA, amplify it and then measure it on a machine that measures the length and amount of whatever you have amplified. You have to amplify it to make it detectable. If you didn't amplify it you would never see it. PCR is the major invention in all of this. Kary Mullis won the Nobel prize for it. Whether you are looking at one location or the whole panel's worth of maybe 15 locations, that's called the genotype. That's the heart of all this. That people basically have unique genotypes, except for identical twins."

He explained how his True Allele technology retrieves singular DNA profiles from mixed samples. "When the computer does its separation, True Allele teases apart the genotypes of the different contributors to the DNA mixture. It doesn't look at any answer, it doesn't know what you are going to compare it with, it basically solves the problem for all possible trillion genotypes. It solves it and then when it's done, it gives an objective answer for each of the locations, for each of the contributors.

"For example, if there are four contributors and there are 15 locations, it's giving you 60 genotypes. And then you take one contributor's genotype from the evidence and then compare it with a reference.

"Only afterwards you get a match statistic called a likelihood ratio which tells you the change in probability from coincidence. If it's the same probability as coincidence there's no information. But if the number is a million times larger that indicates the data is supporting the idea that there is a match to that person. And if it's one in a million or one in a billion times less probable than coincidence then that points away from the person."

Dr Perlin said his company, Cybergenetics, would be willing to test Philip's schoolbag for investigating officers in the hope it might throw up some new evidence which could be used in the case. He said when most scientists test DNA, there are two parts to the test, which includes generating the data and then interpreting it. Most police forensic labs around the world, when evidence involves a mixed sample of three or more people with very low amounts of DNA, struggle to interpret it and the outcome is normally inconclusive. But Dr Perlin says his technology would be able to carry out the analysis on the mixed DNA on Philip's bag within days which could turn out to be crucial to the investigation.

"If there are five or 10 contributors, the computer might take days to think about it. But something easy could be done in a few minutes, like two people can separate very easily. On a handgun, for example, we typically see five people's DNA."

In 2016, convicted paedophile Eamon Cooke was named as a person of interest in the Philip Cairns case.

A sample of DNA was taken from the child abuser on his deathbed to cross-examine against those said to be on the bag. It was reported at the time, after scientific analysis, that it did not match those on the satchel.

When it comes to how many DNA samples are actually on the bag there have been mixed reports. Some newspapers reported in 2016 that there were three separate single profiles obtained by FSI. However, I have been told that it's believed there were only mixed DNA samples.

Dr Perlin pointed out that even if there are single samples of DNA on the shoulder bag and Cooke's is not one of them, there is still the possibility that it could be contained within the mixed samples of DNA if he did in fact touch it. Dr Perlin said by testing the mixed sample and pulling out individual profiles from it, investigators will be able to either conclusively rule Cooke in or out as having touched the bag.

"If they are saying they are seeing a mixture, that means they are not just seeing flat line noise, they are seeing actual signal. Based on that signal, True Allele can separate out the genotypes and produce a match statistic that indicates to what extent his DNA is or isn't present in that mixture. He could be statistically excluded from that as well. If it turns out that he is there, the case is closed and you can move on. You may end up with more evidence that can be used. If they send us the data, we would be more than happy to look at it and perhaps that would bring closure to the family and the case."

In the days that followed the discovery of Philip's bag, an anonymous witness came forward to gardaí claiming to have seen a man in the area that evening. He was described as being in his early twenties, late teens, and was wearing dark clothes and was fairly tall. Despite an appeal for the man in question to come forward, nothing ever came of the alleged sighting. Was this the person who dropped the bag in the laneway or was he merely a local man making his way home?

Supt Frank Hanlon appealed at the time to whoever had left the bag in the lane to come forward. "We feel that this bag may have been dumped by a person who found it because they thought it was too hot to handle. We would be very anxious for that person to come forward and they need not be fearful of the consequences. It's the only contact we have had since the boy went missing."

Catherine said there were many local rumours at the time following the bag's discovery, including that school children were behind Philip's disappearance.

"Initially, everyone thought it was probably kids who had done something wrong and that was the theory for a long time. They had brought the kids at Philip's school back during the mid-term. My younger brother was in Philip's class. So many people were throwing so many theories at it. It's too big, I believe, for it to have been kids because Philip would have been found by now. A lot of people were pointing down towards the River Dodder too but why would he have gone down there? He was a quiet, well behaved young fella."

Catherine had hoped the discovery of the bag would help lead detectives to Philip and she never imagined 35 years later that he would still be missing and his family left still not knowing what happened to him. "It's the only evidence that was ever found. I'm just disappointed that the bag didn't help find him.

"We thought it was going to help and the biggest

disappointment was that it didn't. It's the only damn thing that was found and it didn't help the family."

Speaking of what she personally thinks happened to the teen, Catherine said she believed he was taken in a car as he would have been spotted walking back to the school during such a busy time of day. As a teenager at the time, she would have used the lane in which Philip's bag was found a lot herself. "No matter what lane he would have taken, there were so many people going back to school that day who would have seen him. That's why I believe it was a car he was picked up in."

It must also be noted that the bag was discovered on the same day officers visited Colaiste Eanna. One detective I spoke to said it was still not known whether the visit by detectives prompted the bag to be left in the laneway that evening or not: "It's extremely coincidental to say the least."

Former Detective Sergeant Tom Doyle, who was based at Rathfarnham Garda Station for 18 years, said the bag being found was extremely important and could still one day solve the case.

When Doyle took over the investigation, one of the first things he did was place the fabric bag in an evidence bag in the hope that there would be advancements in DNA testing which would one day lead to Philip's abductor or the person who left the satchel in the lane being tracked down. "The significance of the bag is huge because the lane itself in which it was found had been searched and there was no sign of it. I have even spoken to some of the guards who were involved in that search and they said they walked up and down it several times and it wasn't there. It would have been used on a regular basis and nobody saw anything. It had been raining and the leaves under the bag were wet but the bag itself was dry, so it hadn't been there for a few days. Someone had placed it there.

"It was the first lead and there was a huge interest at the time as to how it would have got there. A lot of examinations were carried out, there were doors knocked upon. Was it put there to throw someone off at the time? Was someone getting too close and it was placed there to throw them off the scent? All of these things go through your mind and all of these things were investigated and looked into. It has never been 100 per cent established as to why it was there and who put it there."

But Doyle said he was hopeful that advancements in DNA technology would indeed one day lead to those who left the bag in the laneway being traced.

He said: "When I got hold of the bag in 1998 I bagged it, tagged it and sealed it all up in the interest that DNA might reach the stage one day where a mixed DNA profile can be broken down into individual profiles. I think they have come a long way towards that but haven't succeeded as of yet.

"If they get to the stage where they can break down that mixed profile into individual profiles it might assist down the line. I heard after I retired that it was analysed again and there was DNA on it but they couldn't establish whose DNA it was. I would feel that there was probably a lot of mixed DNA on that particular bag. The guards at the time would have handled it, the people who found it would have handled it, Philip himself would have handled it. A lot of people would have handled it before it became hugely significant in that there might be something on it that could one day be used. With the advances in DNA, Philip's schoolbag may very well still hold the answer."

Retired Detective John Harrington, who was once a member

of the elite Garda Murder Squad, is also of the belief that DNA on the bag may one day help lead to Philip's abductor being caught or at least finding out what happened to him. "It depends where the bag was after it was first taken possession of. It depends how people handled it. Was it some innocent bypasser who just saw a bag and just threw it in the lane hoping it would help the guards? That could be a theory as well."

Former Garda cold case detective Alan Bailey said there were probably numerous DNA samples now on the bag, including those of officers. But he said the suspect may have left theirs on the bag unwittingly, not realising it would eventually be able to be used to test against years later.

Bailey recalled how the Garda cold case team, which is now known as the Garda Serious Crime Review Team, managed to nab a killer 15 years after a murder due to DNA the culprit had left on some evidence. "The team were looking at a briefcase that was stolen during a robbery and the person who owned it was murdered. We submitted that briefcase for DNA and some 15 years later, DNA that could be used was found on it. Unfortunately, my own DNA was on it because of the way I had handled it too."

Bailey said the hypothesis that a local was possibly involved in Philip's disappearance was highly plausible too as they wouldn't have seemed out of place dropping the bag back in the laneway. "Whoever returned that bag felt comfortable enough that if they were stopped in the area by officers they didn't have to account for what they were doing there.

"That place was awash with police as it was such a strange case for a youngster to disappear like that. It wasn't like the police were there and gone the next day, they were there ongoing. So anyone going back to the area with the missing child's schoolbag would have had to feel very comfortable. They were still running the risk of someone seeing them. That's why it comes back to 'What are you doing here?' and them replying 'Oh, I live locally'."

Meanwhile, retired Detective Inspector Gerry O'Carroll is of the belief that it wasn't a stranger who left the bag in the lane but rather Philip's actual abductor. He does not believe it was an innocent member of the public who just happened to stumble across it. "I would say the killer dropped back the bag. It wasn't a schoolboy out of maliciousness or anyone else. I would say the man who took Philip Cairns dropped that bag back, a red herring job."

But former Detective Sergeant Doyle, who worked on the case up until 2016, believes that the person who left the bag in the laneway may not have been someone who necessarily lived locally but rather knew the neighbourhood well, someone who passed through or frequented the locality occasionally.

"At the time it was considered to possibly be a local person. I believe it was probably someone who frequented the area rather than somebody who actually lived or resided in the area that may have been responsible for putting it back. You also have to look at the possibility that if the person responsible for Philip's disappearance didn't put it back that they may have got someone to leave it back for them for fear of being spotted themself and being asked who they were."

He is certain that there is someone out there who knows who dropped the satchel in the laneway that evening. He also believes that the person or people involved may have been in their teenage years at the time and are now in their late 40s.

Doyle said they may have been asked to leave it back unaware of the bag's importance at the time or were coerced to drop it off. "I'm 100 per cent positive that whoever put that back is very much still alive and I would feel they are probably now approaching 50 years of age, which would put them as mid-teenagers at the time."

The Garda appeals continued over the years for information surrounding the bag. As recently as 2016, Superintendent Peter Duff told a packed press briefing at Tallaght Garda Station how they were still looking to talk to anyone who may have information surrounding Philip's canvas satchel.

"I believe there are people, who were young at the time and may have information in relation to Philip's schoolbag, and for whatever reason did not come forward. I am conscious that following the passage of time and changing circumstances, these people may now be in a position to assist us. I want to reassure anyone who comes forward that they will be treated sensitively and discreetly by investigating gardaí. This may be playing on their minds and I would ask these people to now come forward. For the sake of Mrs Cairns and her family, who have been suffering for 30 years, it is important that we bring this investigation to a conclusion."

Another detective I spoke to subscribed to the opinion that those who dropped the bag may have been manipulated to do it. "They might have been passed the schoolbag and told, 'Go and put that down the laneway and I will buy you sweets in the shop or bring you to McDonald's'. Or on the other hand they may have been threatened with violence if they didn't. If someone young did drop it back, they were probably too young to realise its importance but it's never too late to come forward and say what happened. Philip's family just want answers, to hopefully get their son back. Having to contain a secret of that magnitude must be very hard and it would be a weight lifted off their shoulders too if they came forward and did the right thing."

Philip's younger brother Eoin said the family were left perplexed and confused over the bag being placed in the laneway almost a week after Philip disappeared. And, like his mother, he said the family's hopes were raised upon hearing the news initially. Speaking to *Journal.ie* in November 2015, he said: "We thought it was the big breakthrough. We were kind of thinking, this could be it, we could find him. We were thinking he could be back in his bed that evening. It was a case of waiting – but that hope that he would be found dissipated and weakened over time. We were hoping, but at the same time all we could do was wait. There was a lot of confusion. What to feel? What to think? You felt helpless."

The schoolbag is currently securely stored in a plastic evidence bag in a safe at Rathfarnham Garda Station.

For many detectives who have worked on the case and continue to be involved in the investigation, it holds the key to the case potentially being solved. All the heartbroken Cairns family can do is wait in hope that one day the person or people who left the bag back will find it in their hearts and conscience to come forward and end their years of torture and pain.

The conclusion is that there are three possibilities as to who may have left the satchel in the lane. The first possibility is that it was left there by the person who took Philip. Secondly, that the boy's abductor coerced or threatened someone else, possibly young children, into dropping it off. And thirdly, that a member of the public who happened to stumble across it while out walking left it in the lane, not wanting to be drawn into the investigation. Regardless of who left it there, gardaí are still appealing to that person or people to contact them, confidentially or even anonymously, as it could potentially hold the key to solving the case.

Retired Detective Sergeant Tom Doyle reiterated that the person who left the bag back in the laneway would be treated with the utmost sensitivity and confidentiality if they came forward. "Your call could make the difference and bring peace to Philip's family."

# 6.

# Fact and Fantasy

*'Another bizarre theory was that he wasn't dead, he hadn't been abducted, but that he had been taken because he had shown signs of being the second coming of Christ'*

Within days of Philip being reported missing, theories as to what could have possibly happened to the teenager started to circulate. They ranged from plausible straightforward explanations to downright strange and crazy.

Over the years, Philip's family has had to endure years of distressing and hurtful claims being made about their loved one's disappearance, none of which have ever been proven to be true. Instead, the crazy theories have only compounded the pain the Cairns family are already feeling.

In 2016, Philip's sister Sandra opened up about the hurt that conspiracy theorists were causing the family by discussing his case online. She said they found the hurtful comments being made on social media "deeply disrespectful and disturbing."

Sandra, along with her siblings, have all been deeply impacted by their brother's disappearance and she believes the unfounded speculation about his case could potentially hamper the investigation and deter those who might hold vital information from coming forward.

Not only had there been distressing theories made about her brother, she added, but there had also been a very "callous portrayal" of Philip given, one which bore no resemblance to the boy she knew. "He has been inaccurately described as a troubled, distressed and vulnerable loner. A disturbing narrative has been created which casts a sinister shadow over everything he loved and enjoyed." In fact she said her brother, who had just turned 13 the month before his disappearance, on September 1, was just like any other ordinary teenage boy at the time.

One of the strangest theories which emerged early on in the investigation was that Philip, a smart and well-behaved boy, had gone off willingly to a religious cult.

Just two weeks after the teenager was reported missing, gardaí were drafted in to complete a comb-out of religious cults throughout Ireland over fears he had run off to a sect or was abducted by one. Teams of officers carried out an exhaustive search of temples, churches and shrines belonging to various cults in a bid to find any clues which might connect them to the boy's disappearance.

It was a theory which grew legs and even the gardaí at the time felt the need to follow up on it. Speaking at the time, a Garda spokesman said: "The question of Philip Cairns having been taken by a religious cult has been and still is being pursued. A nationwide check on religious groups is now under way as part of further enquiries into the case." At the time, Philip's father reportedly told the *Evening Herald* newspaper how there was "every possibility" that his son may have been abducted by such a group.

It's believed the theory arose from the simple fact that Philip's family were religious and his mother attended regular prayer meetings. Yet the Catholic Church possessed a lot of power and respect at the time, so the devotion shown by the Cairns family really wasn't out of the ordinary. The schoolboy's mother, who has always been open and honest with the media, said there was nothing to suggest Philip had willingly gone off with one of the religious sects nor been taken by one. "I cannot see what use Philip would be to any group or sect," Alice told a press conference. "If anyone is holding him I appeal to them to let him go."

Many of the officers who worked on the case witnessed at first-hand some of the obscure and, in some cases, crazy hypotheses put forward.

One officer who was caught up in the peculiar theories at the start of the investigation was Detective Inspector Gerry O'Carroll. The former guard said the idea that the schoolboy had been kidnapped by a religious cult or joined a sect was far fetched but that officers were so intent on finding Philip that they looked into every line of enquiry at the time, regardless of how crazy it appeared. Houses of religious sects were searched at the time by officers but to no avail.

O'Carroll said investigating officers even looked into the

possibility that those involved in satanic rituals may have targeted the teenager for being highly religious. At the time, it was also suggested in newspaper reports that there may have been a sect line of enquiry due to the fact that his religion books were found to be missing from his satchel schoolbag which had been dropped in a laneway six days after he was reported missing.

There was an even more extreme theory – the most unusual line of enquiry O'Carroll ever had to investigate during the course of his professional career – that Philip had been abducted in order to be sacrificed to the devil. O'Carroll said he spent a bitterly cold night in November 1986 up the Dublin Mountains with armed officers, waiting in darkness to see if a satanic ritual was about to take place.

He recalled: "One of the most bizarre theories in my entire career, and I was 24 years a detective and involved in over 100 murder investigations, was the information that the child was being sacrificed to the devil.

"I spent the most bizarre night of my whole career waiting with four armed special branch detectives, with submachine guns, for this ghostly procession to be led down by dark cloaked figures from the Hellfire Club.

"We didn't ignore anything. It was bizarre and crazy but we didn't discount any theory. We investigated, as we should have, every theory. It was madness. When I look back at the time I think, 'Christ almighty that was the outer limits, the twilight zone'. It was one of the most bizarre, extraordinary scenes. The Hellfire Club on a nice sunny day is a strange old place but on a November night, with mist coming down the mountains, it was positively macabre."

Officers in Limerick also had to dash to a rundown mill following a call into the incident room that Philip was going to be killed as part of a human sacrifice. "We alerted gardaí in Limerick to go to an old abandoned mill beside Henry Street Garda Station, he was meant to be in there and was going to be killed and sacrificed." But the theory that Philip was kidnapped for a ritual slaughter was quickly ruled out as yet another hoax.

And Chief Superintendent Michael McKeon, who was in charge of the investigation at the time, echoed O'Carroll's thoughts during the early stages of the investigation.

"His mother, we do know, and his family, are deeply religious people and they practise the Catholic religion to a degree that manifests itself by attending meetings and vigils and attending their religious duties in a very positive way. Other than that we have no evidence to show, or reason to believe, that he would have been abducted by any religious sect or would have gone by his own volition to join any sector. "

In November 1986, religious cults expert Don Lydon backed this up and said he believed it was extremely unlikely that Philip was taken by such a group. The psychologist said there were many dangerous sects operating in Ireland at the time and that "disillusioned teenagers are very often tempted into such groups in a frustrated search for 'a more spiritual life'. But he said he was dubious that even the most wicked of cults would be holding Philip. "I would have to ask what use the boy would be to them. In all of these sects, the chief interest is a person's money." He also went on to say that Philip would be too young to 'turn out' on the street, brainwashed into begging or "fundraising".

Within weeks, gardaí had discarded the line of investigation and the outlandish line of enquiry was dropped.

Another strain to the hypothesis circulating at the time – which was also quickly shot down – was that Philip had been kidnapped and was being held against his will by a religious group in mainland Europe. Former cop O'Carroll told me: "Another bizarre theory was that he wasn't dead, he hadn't been abducted, but that he had been taken because he had shown signs of being the second coming of Christ and he was smuggled to the continent, and was being held until he was going to be revealed. There were some extraordinary theories that were coming in. We had a load of clairvoyants and diviners pouring over maps too but nothing ever came of it."

A further allegation was made to gardaí in 1987 that Philip was abducted by a religious sect and taken to Northern Ireland. At the height of the search for the boy, gardaí said they checked out the cults and sects angle "very thoroughly," with investigations in Tramore, Co Waterford, Dublin, Northern Ireland and Donegal yielding nothing.

O'Carroll said that at one stage a man called the gardaí to say he had heard Philip's voice coming from a lake in Co Wicklow. Not from a hidden crevice near the water but from the lake itself, that it was talking to him. "Some fisherman down at the lake in Blessington said he was down there one evening and heard a voice and it said, 'I am Philip Cairns'. This guy reported it to the guards and said he heard a voice telling him, 'I'm here'."

In the following years, the odd religious conspiracy theory still raised its head. In August 1989, almost three years after the teen was reported missing, a man came forward claiming to have met Philip in England and said he had run away to be part of the controversial religious sect, The Moonies.

The former sect member from Co Louth said he had spoken to the teenager at a convention for the cult at Lancaster Gate in North London. He allegedly asked the young boy if he was Philip and he said in response: "Yes, I am Philip Cairns." He also stated at the time to gardaí that the boy said he was safe but did not want to go home. However, in spite of the very elaborate story, nothing ever came of the claim and gardaí later ruled out that it was the missing teen.

Then there was the very odd story of an Irish runaway adolescent in Scotland who claimed he was the missing boy when he was arrested by police officers.

Members of the investigation team from Tallaght Garda Station flew over to interview the young boy who claimed he was Philip, only to discover he was a youngster from Ballymun in North Dublin who bore a vague resemblance to the boy. He's understood to have used Philip's name in a bid to stay out of trouble with the authorities. At the time a detective told the *Sunday World* that they were so hopeful it was the missing teen that they were confident of being able to return Philip home safely to his worried family. "We really felt that this was it, that we were going over to bring Philip back to his parents and his brother and sisters."

Former cold case detective Alan Bailey said another theory that the teenager was abducted by a paedophile ring operating in the area is one which has lingered for some time. The retired officer from New Ross, Co Wexford, who also worked on the brutal Grangegorman murders carried out by Ireland's only serial killer, Mark Nash, said there was no foundation whatsoever to substantiate the claim. Bailey said that for the Cairns family it must be one of the most hurtful speculative theories as it is every parent's worst nightmare.

This has long been a rumour which has circulated amongst some locals in the Rathfarnham area but to date there has been no substantive evidence to back up the claim. "The other theory was that it was a paedophile gang snatching youngsters. They (detectives) were looking at the time but nothing came of it. There is nothing to suggest that was the case because if it was someone operating a ring, they weren't going to rest on the laurels of just taking one child if it had seemed that easy. If they wanted to feed on their fantasies, they would have eventually struck again."

Retired Detective Sergeant Tom Doyle said many people have come forward with unusual theories to him over the years. Doyle spent many hours talking to mediums, diviners and paranormal investigators who wanted to share information they felt was important to the investigation.

He said he took every single one of the offbeat theories and suggestions seriously in case there was an element of truth within them. "Look, you have to respect everybody. People have come forward with various theories. I have spoken to people who read tea leaves and who speak directly with the dead. I have spoken to people whose expertise is in paranormal investigation as well as diviners and people who claim to have a sixth sense."

Doyle said many people came forward with unconventional suggestions over the years as to what had happened to Philip, but unfortunately none of them ever transpired to be credible or of use to the investigation team. "None of these people have ever come forward with one ounce of evidence which would be scientific evidence that you could say was real."

The former officer said he also listened to those with outlandish ideas in case they did in fact know what happened to Philip and were using their offbeat theory as a decoy in order to find out if gardaí were close to cracking the case. "I talked to these people as there was a possibility that they might be seeking information rather than trying to give it. They might have been trying to utilise and use reverse psychology to find out the current stand on the case."

Regardless of all the theories which have been suggested over the years, the Cairns family have always remained extremely dignified despite the untold hurt each one has no doubt caused. They have answered pretty much every question put to them in the vain hope that it would lead to them getting their son and sibling back.

# 7.

# Dark Forces

*'His mind is so twisted and so warped, that he can think to preserve his status by killing his own wife and little adopted baby girl. We can't have someone like that out in society'*

The South Dublin suburb of Rathfarnham where Philip lived, which is neatly positioned between the city and the M50, is regarded by many as a quiet, safe residential area. It's for this reason that the teenager's disappearance really shocked the public in 1986. The area, which is south of Terenure and east of Templeogue, is not, and was not, known for being an area ravaged by crime.

With a population of roughly 18,000 people, Rathfarnham is where professional golfer Padraig Harrington and famous film director Lenny Abrahamson grew up. But despite its quiet location, there have been a number of distressing crimes which have taken place in the leafy suburb over recent years.

One of the most recent stories to hit the headlines in Rathfarnham was the brutal murder of Patricia O'Connor at the family home in 2017. On the evening of her killing on May 29, nine people were living in the cramped four-bed property at Mountain View Park. The former partner of Mrs O'Connor's daughter, Kieran Greene, was later found guilty of killing her after presenting himself at Rathfarnham Garda Station. The distressed man told an officer how he had done "something terrible." He would later tell officers how he struck the grandmother with a hurley during a fight in the bathroom. In a Garda interview he said he was in the bathroom when the retired hospital worker walked in and hit him with a hurl, saying: "Get out, get out." In his account to officers he said that he then grabbed the hurl from her and hit her back. He said he could not recall what happened next but when he woke up there was blood everywhere and he panicked.

The killer is believed to have forensically cleaned the crime scene before moving Mrs O'Connor's body to a bedroom while he tried to figure out what to do next. He later admitted to guards that he first buried the grandmother in a shallow grave in a field an hour's drive away in County Wexford, before returning to chop up the body with a hacksaw and placing the cut-up remains in plastic bags and throwing them away at various locations around the Dublin and Wicklow Mountains. He was worried that a farmer might have stumbled across her buried body and contacted the authorities.

The 61-year-old victim had initially been reported as

missing by her family. But the grizzly truth would soon emerge when on June 10, 2017, a family having a picnic close to the Sally Gap in Co Wicklow stumbled across her torso, which was described in court as looking like animal remains. Witness Christine Murphy said they "came across something" over a bank at the side of the road at Old Boley.

On the same day, in a case of extraordinary coincidence, two people out walking at Glenmacnass Waterfall in Co Wicklow saw what they thought were animal organs on a rock but they were human remains and belonged to the caring grandmother. It would emerge at the trial that in total 15 body parts were found over a 30km radius at nine locations in both the Dublin and Wicklow Mountains.

The 61-year-old's remains were initially thought to be that of a male due to the measurements of the bones found. The court heard how the woman, described by her son as a "determined lady", had died from blunt force trauma to the head. Former deputy State pathologist Dr Michael Curtis said he found the deceased's head had been struck a minimum of three times with a solid implement.

Although Greene initially claimed responsibility for the brutal killing, in December 2017 he amended his version of events and actually placed the blame on the deceased woman's husband, Gus O'Connor, telling officers he had killed her and that Keith Johnston had dismembered the body. He claimed he was "set up" to take the blame.

While Greene was handed a life sentence for the brutal murder of his mother-in-law, several members of the victims family were also convicted for trying to conceal the killing. The victim's daughter, Louise O'Connor, granddaughter

Stephanie O'Connor and Louise O'Connor's former partner and father of Stephanie, Keith Johnston, were found guilty of impeding the apprehension or prosecution of Greene, knowing or believing him to have murdered Mrs O'Connor. The grandmother's husband, Augustine 'Gus' O'Connor, also pleaded guilty to reporting his wife as a missing person, knowing she was already dead.

It would also emerge during the trial that the victim's granddaughter had disguised herself to look like her grandmother on the night of her alleged murder in a bid to give the impression that the deceased woman was still alive. The 23-year-old was sentenced to two years in prison, with six months suspended for her role in the sickening plot to cover up the murder. She was found guilty on a single charge of impending the apprehension or prosecution of her father, who had bludgeoned her grandmother to death. The jury accepted she had disguised herself as Mrs O'Connor as "a ruse" to pretend she was still alive.

Another upsetting case to make the headlines over recent decades was the horrific double murder carried out by Frank McCann. The former swimming coach is currently one of Ireland's longest serving prisoners after brutally murdering his wife Esther and their 18-month-old foster daughter Jessica by deliberately setting fire to the family home on September 4, 1992. It is believed he carried out the horrific act in order to stop his wife from finding out about a child he had fathered with a 17-year-old girl with special needs who he was training at swimming.

A complaint about McCann's relationship with the girl, alleging he had fathered a child with her, was reportedly made by the teenager's mother to the Adoption Board on April 17, 1991. She had given birth to a baby girl during the summer of 1987 who was later put up for adoption. It would later transpire that the baby was born shortly after McCann had married Esther O'Brien, a native of Tramore, Co Waterford, on May 22, 1987. The late Father Michael Cleary, who was a friend of the girl's family, represented her during discussions with McCann and an anonymous payment of £500-£600 was allegedly made to the teen mother's father.

Just before the brutal killings, McCann was undergoing a background check as he had made an application to adopt Jessica. The toddler, who was born in 1991, was the daughter of Frank's own adopted sister Jeanette, who grew up with him and his brothers and parents in the nearby area of Terenure. She had asked McCann and Esther to adopt Jessica shortly after her birth in March 1991. McCann, who worked as a publican but also coached swimmers within the Irish Olympic set-up, feared his dark secret would be exposed following unexpected delays in the adoption process and is understood to have instead murdered his family to cover it up and stop his wife from finding out. It would later transpire that the Adoption Board had notified the McCann solicitor of its final decision on July 28, 1992, but gardaí believe McCann was already aware of this development.

The twisted killer went about murdering his young family by setting off a gas cylinder and blowtorch at the family home on Butterfield Avenue when he went to work at a Blessington pub in Co Wicklow. At about 2am the fire engulfed the house. McCann then tried to fool everybody by arriving back at the horrific scene and playing the part of an anguished father desperately trying to rescue his family from the blazing inferno. It would later emerge during his trial how he even stood in the garden shouting "Esther" and "my baby" as the house burned down in front of him. Neighbours raised a ladder to the front bedroom window in a bid to save Esther and Jessica as the emergency services arrived. McCann is said to have had to be restrained by neighbours as he put on another false display of anguish as he reached for the ladder.

Esther, who had suffered extensive burns, died from the inhalation of smoke which included carbon monoxide while little Jessica, who still had a soother in her mouth when her body was discovered, died in her cot. The court heard from the prosecution during McCann's court case how they believe he drove back to Rathfarnham from the Blessington pub, a journey of about 20 minutes, and started the fire in the hallway area of the house. The combination of a gas cylinder and a blowtorch, the prosecution said, resulted in a "a fast, ferocious fire in a very short period of time".

More shocking details about McCann trying to kill Esther and little Jessica prior to the brutal murder would later emerge, including first cutting the brake lines of his wife's car. In a separate incident, he is believed to have caused an electric blanket on her bed to catch fire by stripping back electrical wires within it. Luckily, Esther was woken by a phone ringing and found the blanket, which had been folded in four on the foot of the bed, in flames. The scheming killer thought ahead and got rid of the blanket so officers investigating the case would be unable to later examine it.

McCann then also tried to spark a massive gas leak at their home. In July 1992, four separate gas leaks were reported at the family home. During one particular gas leak on July 28, 1991, Esther awoke to smell gas and quickly left the house. She even carefully pushed the car down the driveway, before ringing McCann at the pub he was working in at the time. After the killer phoned the gas company to complain of a smell of gas, a fitter arrived at 7.55am and discovered a colossal presence of gas which was the result of two gas joints completely parting. It was stated at the time that the damage could have only happened after heat had been applied to the joints and they were prised apart. It would only be on his fourth attempt that he would manage to fulfil his sick plan of killing them.

The calculated murderer was charged in April 1993 but tried to take his own life during his first trial by reportedly setting fire to himself at Arbour Hill Prison, so the jury was dismissed and the trial halted. But his second trial in 1996 resulted in McCann being sentenced to two concurrent life sentences.

In May 2019, the killer was given his first taste of freedom when he was allowed to take part in a course at Ballyfermot College in Dublin. He walked out of Arbour Hill Prison in Dublin city centre, which is just a stone's throw away from the Criminal Courts of Justice (CCJ), and got a bus which brought him to Chapelizod five kilometres away, where he went by foot the remainder of the way. It is believed he was studying a 10-week-long computer course at the time. A source told me how McCann was waiting for Covid lockdown restrictions to be lifted so he could take part in another training course at the same college.

At the time of writing this book, he had been transferred from Arbour Hill Prison to Mountjoy. The 61-year-old is currently due for parole. But his own family, as well as his victims, have spoken publicly about why he should never be released. In March 2021, his sister-in-law, Elizabeth Shorten, urged Minister for Justice, Helen McEntee, not to approve his release. She said the killer should never be allowed to walk free as he still poses a danger to society. "His mind is so twisted and so warped, that he can think to preserve his status by killing his own wife and little adopted baby girl. We can't have somebody like that out in society."

Ms Shorten, who is married to the killer's younger brother Derek, had recalled how they only found out about the tragedy after returning from their honeymoon. "He has no moral gauge to say that what he has done is wrong, so there is nothing to stop him, should the circumstances not go his way, to repeating those offences again," Ms Shorten said. "He has never shown any remorse for what he has done." And she said on the radio how evil would "walk free" if he was paroled, and said both families, including his wife Esther's, would "spend the rest of our lives hoping he doesn't do something like this again."

McCann, who was once vice-president of the Irish Amateur Swimming Association (IASA) and president of the Leinster Swimming Association, was also a close friend of swim coach Derry O'Rourke, who it would later emerge was a prolific paedophile. They lived within walking distance to each other in Rathfarnham. Along with O'Rourke, McCann also spent time with George Gibney, who trained some of the country's best swimmers, but fled the country after being accused of 27 counts of rape and sexual abuse of minors. Both men are understood to have regularly visited McCann's home in Rathfarnham. No charges of sexual abuse against a minor were ever brought against McCann.

Father-of-six O'Rourke was jailed in 1998 for 12 years for sexual assault, indecent assault and statutory rape of children. He then received further sentences in 2000 and 2005 for sexual abuse of minors between the 1970s and 1992. He was handed a further 10-year sentence for the rape and indecent assault of another girl he trained.

During the court case, Paddy McCarthy SC, prosecuting, told Mr Justice Carney how the complainant made a statement to gardaí in 1999 following media coverage of O'Rourke's 1998 convictions. He said she had difficulty coming to terms with the offences, which occurred while she was a promising swimmer between the ages of 14 and 18. Detective Sergeant Sarah Keane added that the girl in question had been a boarding pupil at the school during the 1970s and came under the twice-daily coaching of O'Rourke. She said in 1975, O'Rourke met her each evening in a boiler room, with the door locked, to discuss training and would touch her over and under her clothes. The following year he had an office and would make her sit on his knee and would take off her underwear and penetrate her digitally and with a vibrator.

Det Sgt Keane said the girl believed that the abuse was an integral part of her training. The child abuser used "relaxation" sessions of massage to make the girl lie naked on the floor while he digitally penetrated her, performed oral sex on her and masturbated himself. He also made her swim naked and would get into the pool to rub up against her.

The brave survivor told the court in her victim impact statement the unbearable pain the abuse had caused her over the years. "This is my tsunami," she said, and added: "It has taken all my determination to deal with the hurt, pain, sadness and anger, and turn the tide of destructive forces that have arisen from what you did to me." O'Rourke, who had moved from Rathfarnham to Edenderry, Co Offaly, pleaded guilty to 29 charges relating to 11 girls and covering offences of sexual assault, indecent assault and unlawful carnal knowledge of girls under the age of 15, from 1976 to 1992. The full indictment had a total of 90 charges. Sentences were imposed on 27 charges, totalling 109 years with the longest terms being two of 12 years for unlawful carnal knowledge.

After he was sentenced, Olympic medallist Michelle Smith de Bruin questioned why nobody had raised concerns over his inappropriate behaviour. "Why did no one question if he should be allowed to take young girls on their own into the gym in the dark to hypnotise them, or to the pool for special attention? Why did no one question when he made lewd comments about the young girls?"

O'Rourke was released from the Midlands Prison in Portlaoise on March 1, 2007. As with all Irish inmates, he was entitled to have 25 per cent remission of his sentence for good behaviour. His current whereabouts are unknown.

Another paedophile who operated in close proximity to Rathfarnham was John McClean.

The former Terenure College rugby coach was a prolific child abuser who was convicted of abusing 23 men over a 17-year period. He was handed an 11-year sentence with three years suspended for his crimes at the elite all-boys secondary school. The former English teacher systematically abused young pupils there from 1973 to 1990. McClean took advantage of his trusted position as a rugby coach and would threaten to kick his victims off the team as a means to manipulate them.

In February 2021, Court 13 at the Dublin District Court heard from one of his victims how McClean, of Casimir Avenue, Harold's Cross, Dublin, had destroyed his life. The 76-year-old sat silently in court with his head down and would not look at the many victims he had abused over the years who had turned up to watch justice finally being served on him. The remaining victims, who did not wish to read out their statements themselves, sat quietly as prosecuting counsel Paul Murray read them into the record after each charge carried out by McClean was read out.

The paedophile, who started teaching at Terenure College at the age of 21 in 1966, admitted to abusing his first victim in 1973. McClean, who would discuss his twisted fantasies with his targets, used to prowl the secondary school corridors searching out his next victim. If he found a schoolboy standing outside a classroom door for misbehaving he would take them away and physically beat and sexually abuse them. He carried out both pre-planned and opportunistic attacks on boys and would choose those who he deemed gentle and unlikely to resist. One boy alone is reported to have been abused 36 times by the paedophile. And it emerged that at least two of McClean's victims had been sexually abused at Terenure primary school, the feeder school for the secondary college. The pervert was so brazen in his abuse that following his horrific acts of sexual assault he would befriend his victims' parents and talked his way into their homes. One victim said: "It was galling to see him welcomed in our family home. This man knew no shame."

Many of McClean's victims ended up suffering from depression and anxiety due to the sickening acts inflicted upon them, with some even attempting to take their own lives as the trauma of the abuse was too much for them to handle. Although McClean pleaded guilty to 27 charges of child abuse, there was a total of 99 incidents. The "monster in disguise", as one of his victims described him, was reported for abuse as far back as 1979 to at least one Carmelite priest but he refused to believe it to be true and so years of horrific child abuse followed. After he left his position at Terenure College he went on to become the Director of Rugby at University College Dublin (UCD) and only retired in 2011.

When quizzed by gardaí about the abuse and shown black and white photos of his victims, McClean denied even knowing them, yet alone destroying their lives, and when asked about the individuals he said they "mean nothing to me" and even accused some of them of making the abuse up. He even had the audacity to tell detectives investigating the claims: "No, I don't think I did any of those things, nothing is familiar."

When being sentenced, Judge Pauline Codd praised his many victims for their "immense courage and strength". One survivor said: "I will never forgive or forget what he did. He ruined my life when he was supposed to be protecting me."

Survivor Damien Hetherington, who was abused while trying to retrieve a copybook during a class in 1973, said everybody knew about McClean and what he was up to at the time but did nothing about it. "The dogs in the street were barking about this particular individual for the 30 years he was there but he was still left there." He added: "The thing is, he's exposed now, he got what he deserves, and I would encourage any more victims to please come forward, it's never too late. This has been a scar on this country for God knows how long. Not just the clergy, teachers and that but sports and everything.

But for anyone else please come forward, you'd be surprised how good you'll feel."

Another convicted child abuser who lived in Rathfarnham was a man who was handed a life sentence for raping a young male in 2002. He also admitted to sexually assaulting three other teenage boys at his home as well as at hotels around Ireland between 1989 and 2000. He cannot be named for legal reasons. While serving his sentence he was also handed a five-year sentence for producing child pornography.

One man who knew the paedophile in the mid-1980s, but who does not wish to be named, said the pervert used to sell radio transmitters to young teenage boys in the Leinster area who were trying to set up pirate radio stations. And he said he even bought some from him in 1986.

He told me: "I heard an advert by him on the radio as a 13-year-old boy in 1986 and I rang him at 5.30pm on a Tuesday and by 7pm he was at my parents' front door. He was waiting by the phone obviously to be out to me that quickly. He could jump in his car and be anywhere in a very short time. He was only interested in 13 and 14-year-old boys I believe. Once they got past that age, he wasn't interested. Thankfully, he never abused me. We were all kids running pirate radio stations and if there was a problem with some of the equipment he would drop over and fix it. He befriended a lot of young teenage boys."

# 8.

# Prime Suspect

*'He really was a Pied Piper-type character. He was a complete sleazebag. If there was ever someone wearing a sign with 'paedo' written on it, it was him'*

By the late Seventies, Eamon Cooke had become a minor celebrity after getting involved with pirate station Radio Dublin. But unbeknown to his adoring fans he also possessed a dark, sinister side. The scruffy DJ was also a prolific paedophile. Many people now believe he was using the popular station as a front to lure children into his clutches.

Nobody ever suspected at the time that Cooke, with his confident radio demeanour and public persona, was the monster he would later emerge to be. Not only would he later be convicted and accused of abusing many children, the paedophile would also become the only person to ever publicly be named as a possible suspect in the Philip Cairns investigation. No other individual has ever openly been identified as a person of interest in the case.

Cooke was not your stereotypical radio star. Scrawny in appearance, he was not squeaky clean or well turned out. The chain-smoking broadcaster didn't care much for personal hygiene and in fact rarely appeared to wash. He also let his yellow, grubby fingernails grow long. The skinny grey-haired DJ never used an ashtray and instead would just let the ash from his cigarettes fall all over his jumper. The result of which meant he constantly smelt of stale smoke. Combined with bad body odour, it was enough to turn even the strongest of stomachs.

Cooke also had the habit of not changing his clothes and would sometimes wear the same shirt for days on end, resulting in a filthy black dirt line forming around the rim of his collar. He once claimed that he only used a sponge and water to clean himself as he never had time for a bath. His drab monotone voice wasn't exactly radio-friendly either. But his ego knew no bounds and his broadcasts would always be presaged by his own 'Captain's Address'.

Despite all this, Cooke's popularity and that of Radio Dublin grew very quickly. Unlike state broadcaster RTE who played middle-aged fare, the DJ favoured pop music which was a huge hit with teenage listeners. The paedophile himself even boasted about the station's popularity years later. "The radio station took off overnight, wiping out RTE radio listenership and doing serious damage to RTE television audience figures." Every weekend, youngsters across the capital would sit around their radios and tune into the 253 frequency to hear their favourite songs being played. Nothing was off limits, from the Bee Gees to The Rolling Stones. Cooke was a qualified electrician who had come from a poor working-class background, so was loving the attention his new-found fame had brought him. The DJ had been branded the new 'Godfather' of pirate radio, a title he relished.

But Cooke never really had an interest in being a DJ before he got involved with Radio Dublin. It was a chance encounter with founder Don Moore which led him down the road of being a radio presenter.

Recalling the day he met the then owner of Radio Dublin, Cooke wrote: "On a winter's evening in 1976 a man called to our shop on Thomas Street with what looked like a piece of junk and asked if I could repair it.

"He said it was a transmitter and was running Radio Dublin, a pirate radio station. I knew nothing about transmitters or pirate radio but said I would have a look at the thing.

"The man was Don Moore. The equipment lay in the shop for months while I tried to learn about transmitters and eventually I got the thing working. Mr Moore called for it and asked me to come up to the radio station which was in his bedroom in Killala Road in Cabra.

"In those days, pirate stations moved every week to avoid detection by the Dept of Posts and Telegraphs. Don Moore's house was raided and soon after this, while I was there, the equipment was dismantled.

"Since it was a homemade piece of equipment, it broke down often and Don Moore would be back on to me. I would go to the station, fix it up and be gone.

"At that time, the only broadcasts on the station were late on Wednesday nights and on Sunday afternoons, and this continued right up to December '77. In April 1977, Don Moore's radio station was raided while it was broadcasting. By now I went along to the station broadcasts each Sunday. Don wanted to charge listeners 50p each week for a club membership but I insisted it was a listeners' station and it would be better to get commercial advertising. We fell out over this and on the 27th of July 1977 I set up Radio Dublin in my sitting room at 3 Sarsfield Road."

Cooke loved being seen as the local hero and would often boast about spending large sums of money on toys for local disadvantaged children. He liked to paint the impression he cared for the local community by bringing bags of gifts down to kids in the local orphanages. Years later he talked of spending cash on "children in homes and orphanages, food parcels for down-and-out families and hiring buses to bring whole orphanages out to the zoo and other places for the day". At the time people were not aware of the possible alternative motive behind his generosity – to get as close to as many vulnerable children as possible. There is no proof he abused any child he gifted with toys or sweets at any of the orphanages or hospitals he visited but for many, including those who knew him and some of his victims, the mere thought of him even being in their presence is enough to turn their stomachs.

The DJ's public persona bore a striking similarity to another famous child abuser – English broadcaster Jimmy Savile. Both radio celebrities drove flashy cars – Cooke a silver Jaguar and Savile a Rolls-Royce – and used their fame to gain people's trust so their unusual behaviour around children would go unnoticed. Those who tried to raise concerns were quickly deterred or intimidated to stay quiet.

Like chain-smoking Cooke, Savile, who was rarely seen without a giant cigar in his mouth, also used his fame to prey on young kids and often visited sick children in hospitals. An official inquiry carried out following his death in 2011 found the late Top of the Pops host had abused a staggering 60 children but the unofficial number is believed to have been closer to 500.

It has even been claimed that the pair crossed paths on a number of occasions with Savile visiting Cooke at his studio in Inchicore during the late Seventies. It has been well publicised over the years that the British TV star enjoyed his trips to Ireland and would travel over annually during the late Seventies and early Eighties to take part in charity events. The blonde-haired Jim'll Fix It presenter, whose name was associated with many charities in Ireland too, was even awarded the Cross of Office of Merit by the Sovereign Military Order of Malta in Dublin in November 1977.

A former DJ at Radio Dublin, who was 16 at the time, recalled seeing Savile in the studios in 1979. The man who witnessed the two men meeting, and who asked not to be identified, spoke to *Hotpress Magazine* in June 2016. "There's plenty of stuff online about Savile coming across to do charity events, but nothing that mentions that he used to publicise them on Radio Dublin.

"I have vivid memories of Savile coming into the studios to plug a walk he was doing from the city centre to Portmarnock for the Central Remedial Clinic, which was about 10k. You got your sponsorship card and walked with Jimmy. This would have been either the Easter or June Bank Holiday in 1979, possibly a little earlier, when the station was still broadcasting from No 3 Sarsfield Road in Inchicore.

"I'm not sure what the exact nature of their relationship was, but knowing what we know now, you can't help but wonder, 'Did they get up to anything together?' It's horrible to think that there are probably people out there who were abused by Cooke, but are still too traumatised to talk about it."

At the time, he went on to say, child abuse was just not something which was discussed. "This was Ireland in 1978. I was 16 – we didn't know anything about paedophiles. Adults preying on a child just wasn't discussed, which of course suited Cooke down to the ground." Did they know of each other's sordid abuse of children? Did they target kids together when Savile was in Ireland? Or were they just merely two radio presenters who happened to know each other?

The disc jockey said Cooke was so paranoid about security at the station that he had steel doors fitted throughout the three-bedroom house where it was located. "When the station was in Sarsfield Road, I had a key to get in and open the hall door. There was another key hidden inside, which opened the steel door that got you into the little kitchen/dining room where the phone was. There was another steel door that led up the stairs to Cooke's bedroom, which someone said was electrified. He definitely ran cables to the back door and told An Post, "Come in and you'll be electrocuted!" One or two mornings there'd be a note asking me to wake him up, usually because he was attending a court case."

One thing he recalled was how the entire house was absolutely filthy. "The first time I knocked on his bedroom door and went in, I thought someone had died. I used the bathroom one day and noticed lice control stuff there for his head. A lot of the dirt was down to the fact that he was always digging. When we moved from Sarsfield to 58 Inchicore Road, he asked An Post to re-route Radio Dublin's famous 758684 phone-line. They said 'no chance', so he dug a fucking trench on the railway track from the back of No 3 to No 58, overnight or maybe over two nights. I don't know whether he studied the train timetables but this was incredibly dangerous."

Cooke himself described how overcrowded the house was and how disorganised the Radio Dublin studio was. "This was not a radio station as many would imagine it with well laid out studios. There were two record players, a tape recorder and a microphone all connected up with lots of wires pushed up against the sitting room window. There was a small sofa and a piano in the room which was around the same size as the dining room. The presenter sat in front of this jumble of wires. His 'producer' – for want of a better word – sat in the corner with the next record ready."

The lack of seclusion at the clutter-filled house used to annoy him. "Privacy in the house was a thing of the past. Even with a steel door on the stairs, people had to be given a key to get to the toilet and it was normal for Joan (former wife) and I to go to bed and have someone wake me in the early hours after pulling out some wire or doing something which put the radio station off air.

"The back bedroom, now full of junk, had an old table near the window with the transmitter and other equipment on it. A transmitter today is a unit in a steel case. In those days there were no steel cases for equipment. Large glass tubes glowed red. Bare wires fixed on top of them carried up to 4,000 volts – 220 volts is normal household voltage and that is lethal, so the door to the room was always locked. Even with all the precautions, I ended up in hospital twice with severe electric burns from touching the equipment long after it was switched off."

Cooke moved his studios to another property, 58 Inchicore Road, in 1979. He claimed years later that he needed more space to operate the growing station. "In late 1979 I found a new premises for the radio station. The house was no longer viable for the number of people coming and going each day. It was an old abandoned bungalow on Inchicore Road, only a quarter of a mile from Sarsfield Road. The cost was £39,000. The station's bank account had nearly £30,000 but the remainder took months to get. Staff opted to go without wages for a long time and a few old friends came up with money. I don't know the date we started up at 58 Inchicore Road but the first broadcast there was on the day the Pope was in the Phoenix Park. We could see everything with binoculars from our new station. I was so cold watching that I developed pneumonia and was in bed in that damp house for a week."

Some of Cooke's victims, who have themselves branded Cooke as the 'Irish Jimmy Savile', also believe that like the notorious BBC DJ he abused hundreds of kids, despite only being prosecuted for two of them. Many believe he purposely put himself in a trusted position at the studio so he could have easy access to young children. As one of his victims, Siobhan Kennedy-McGuinness, told me: "He was able to hide in plain sight."

Teenagers and young kids flocked to the home studio when

it was first set up in the messy sitting room at Sarsfield Road. As the months and years went by and the station's popularity grew, young aspiring DJs including RTE stalwarts Marty Whelan and Dave Fanning became part of the line-up.

Cooke went from broadcasting just a couple of days a week to seven with each presenter getting a two-hour slot. Local kids would make their way into the dishevelled house through the back garden, although some would knock on the front door to ask the sexual predator as well as other innocent unsuspecting DJs working at the station if they wanted anything from the local corner shop.

Young teenage girls, who were eager to be involved in the cool pirate radio station, happily volunteered to answer the two busy phone lines. On extremely busy days in the studio, up to four teenage girls would be on duty answering calls up until 10pm, surrounded by old telephones and discarded television sets.

In his own words, years later, Cooke himself described how kids were always hanging around the house and studio. "From the time the radio station started off daytime broadcasts in December '77 to the time the back of the house was boarded up in January '78 was probably three weeks or so. During this time children and teenagers called non-stop to the house, most to the front door to see the station or have requests played. Local children came into the house through the back garden or to the front door to ask for requests or to know if anyone wanted anything in the local shop. Usually someone wanted something and the children were told to keep the change."

Radio Dublin was a pirate station and Cooke is said to have loved the fact he was breaking the law. Gardaí were always trying to find out where the studio was located and shut it down. In fact, it was raided twice in 1978. The first time it was searched was in January of that year and a lot of equipment was removed but Cooke somehow managed to put the station back on air.

As much as he loathed the law he was also obsessed by it, according to many of those who knew him. During his time at Radio Dublin, Cooke had his Silver Jaguar car radio tuned in so he could listen in on the Garda frequency. Unlike today, it was easy to find on the wireless with the right know-how. He quickly started to annoy authorities, though, as he would often arrive at crime scenes before they did. And the more gruesome the crime, the better.

One detective told me how he saw himself as a crime fighter and in unearthed documents I have obtained, he wrote how he would follow and tackle criminals before the gardaí had even arrived. "I had bought an old grey Jaguar for security work and had a radio tuned to the Garda channels. I soon had an unofficial Garda call sign of Alpha 7 and newspapers started to write about our activities. It would take a whole book to detail these activities, many of them were covered by newspapers, including ramming stolen cars, taking on armed robbers and disposing of drug stashes."

He even admitted to breaking the law himself while tackling these criminals. "Our methods were what we like to call unique but others said they were totally illegal. There was uproar once when we followed a drug dealer, found his drugs hidden on the Greenhills Road and threw them on the Dodder. Thousands of fish died," he boasted.

And in an article in the *Sunday People* in 1972, Cooke posed in his car while boasting about his crime-fighting skills. He claimed he had been working as a patrolman for the past four years and before meeting the journalist for the interview, had investigated a break-in, a knife fight and a warehouse alarm in the space of just two hours. He said his "shifts" began at 10pm and ended at around 3am.

Cooke claimed he first started to help out the gardaí when his shop on Thomas Street in Dublin's city centre was broken into several times. "I decided to keep watch until I caught some of those responsible. I got two, but more kept coming. Finally, I thought that if I couldn't snare them I'd patrol the city and arrest others of the same type. Mind you, I never bite off more than I can chew. If I'm likely to get the worst of a scrap I let the villains get away. When cornered they can be vicious."

Speaking of one of his dangerous pursuits, he bragged about a death-defying chase along a rooftop. "I was dead scared I'd fall but they were as agile as monkeys and got away." Or the time he helped a squad car to block a road. "The stolen car headed straight towards me but I felt sure it would stop or swerve. It came straight on through and sliced off part of the front of my car. There was a fair bit of damage but I soon got the car back on the road."

In 1973, a letter appeared in the *Sunday Independent* accusing Cooke of being a police informer. The letter from a person going by the name K.Grace, along with a picture of the DJ, bore the headline: 'Stop being a snooper!'

In the article body of the piece itself, it stated: "I would like to give this advice to Eamon Cooke, stop being a snoop for the Gardaí, they are well able to do their own snooping. And Eamon, if you make one slight mistake, you will get your summons in spite of all your goody, goody work. You're not smart, you're only an informer."

Although he openly boasted of being able to take on hardened criminals, Cooke was far from athletic and as a child went to judo classes in a bid to learn how to defend himself. In documents I have seen, which were penned by the abuser himself, he claims that as a boy he tried to learn boxing but gave up after being hit far too many times and receiving serious injuries. "At around 12 there was a minor incident that was to change much of my life. I was in a friendly boxing match in school and got a broken nose which I never attended to. I did not have reactions fast enough for boxing so I was determined that this would not happen again. I spent all of my pocket money for the next year in learning judo. Many times I came home with black eyes and teeth missing to tell my mother I fell. I always told my dad later what happened but my mother was the sort who worried too much so I didn't tell her. A year later I could handle myself before anyone but never needed to do so.

"I developed permanent sinus problems from the broken nose. When it became obvious I was going to have problems with my nose for the rest of my life, the doctor said I would be better off letting my nails grow and clearing out my nose with these each day. It may sound disgusting but it has worked for the past 50 years now and, in time, I got to be proud of my long nails even though I seldom cleaned them."

James Dillon, former station manager at Radio Dublin, said Cooke was a loner who seemed to like the station because it was illegal, not for the love of the music itself. "Everything about him just seemed devious." Dillon said he never once suspected Cooke to be the evil child abuser he would later emerge to be.

He said despite the DJ always being surrounded by children, it never registered with him as being strange. This was due partly to the location of the studio, which was in a busy residential area of Dublin. It was not in a bustling city centre but rather on a normal suburban street. "If the station had been located in the city centre then maybe it would have been odd but as it was in the middle of a housing estate it didn't seem that strange. Kids were always coming in and out. The younger ones were often there with their older sisters," he said.

Dillon said he was shocked when a fellow member of staff approached him one night to tell him Cooke had been accused of molesting a young child who was a frequent visitor to the studio. The DJ was in utter disbelief and struggled to get his head around the sickening allegations. He wanted to hear the horrific claims first-hand from the victim's own mouth for himself. The little nine-year-old girl, Siobhan Kennedy-McGuinness, lived just a few doors down from the studio in Inchicore. She had told an older female friend that the radio star was "doing things to her" which was later relayed back to one of the station's staff members.

A plan was hatched for the older girl to record Siobhan as she recalled once again the incident involving Cooke. Dillon said he wanted to determine exactly what had happened as the extremely damaging claims would not only see the end of Cooke's career if true, but would also mean the end of the station. "We decided to take one of the small tape recorders and go back and talk to the girl. We went with the recorder and the girl opened up and talked away. The content of the conversation sounded innocent to a degree, she talked and kind of giggled about a banana."

Enraged staff members, who were sickened by what they had heard, decided they needed further proof to back up the young girl's claims before confronting Cooke. And so they set upon searching every inch of the studio while the broadcaster was away on holiday in Spain in April 1978. Much to their horror, they discovered a stash of Polaroid photos showing young children in their underwear.

The bundle of pictures were not overtly sexual but were enough for them to determine Cooke was up to no good and was using the innocent young children for his own perverted sexual gratification. The broadcaster had managed to obtain the sickening images by blackmailing the children who were in them, it would later emerge. The new discovery sickened Dillon to the core and, along with the vast majority of other DJs at the station, he decided he could no longer work for Cooke. He couldn't help wondering if the dirty middle-aged man had been using him as well as other young, hip DJs at the station as a magnet to lure innocent kids into the studio.

He would later learn of the sickening level of intimidation Cooke would use against the young children in the images in order to keep his sordid acts a secret. "The girls could go anywhere in the house and sometimes Eamon would be upstairs with them and he used to take photographs of them in their underwear. He would then say to them, "Your mammy wouldn't like to see you in your underwear in my house, sure she wouldn't?" I thought to myself, 'this is an adult manipulating a child and he has to be doing it for the wrong reasons'. From that second, I knew he was 100 per cent guilty. What exactly he was doing wasn't the point. What level of touching or abuse didn't matter."

For Dillon and other staff members at the station, the images were enough to corroborate the young girl's story. When Cooke returned from his holiday he was confronted at Dublin Airport by Dillon and other members of staff about the sickening allegations. He was also told Radio Dublin had been shut down and the majority of its staff had jumped ship and were now working for rival station Big D. Cooke was furious and in the days and weeks which followed carried out a terrifying campaign of terror on a number of staff members who had left. "When Cooke started intimidating the staff, and I mean following them, sitting outside their houses, that kind of stuff, I went to him and said, 'I believe that you are abusing the nine-year-old and I believe you brought all this on yourself. You have to stop intimidating the staff because I'm not going to stand for it'," Dillon recalled.

In response, the man who had become known as Captain Cooke issued a terrifying veiled death threat against him. Remembering verbatim the menacing altercation, Dillon said Cooke knew exactly what he was implying and hoped his words would ward him off trying to find out any more about the alleged abuse. He said Cooke told him: "I will see you six feet under." He responded to Cooke by asking: "Are you threatening to kill me?" to which he quickly changed his tune and said: "Ah no, I'm just saying you are getting yourself very upset. You will end up in an early grave. You are getting too upset about something that's none of your business." It would be the last face-to-face conversation Dillon would ever have with the child abuser. Cooke had a way of intimidating people without it sounding like a threat. He was smart with words in that way, according to those whose paths he crossed.

The walkout by staff and their sabotage of the station transmitter made national headlines. Despite the allegations, Cooke somehow managed to get the station back on air and broadcasting resumed to normal with new DJs and staff replacing the 20 people who had left. Cooke recalled years later what he believed had happened to the radio station while he was on holiday. "Within an hour of us leaving for Spain, Radio Dublin was shut down. All equipment was destroyed, tapes wiped and hundreds of invoices and other papers burnt in the back garden."

In a bid to save his reputation, Cooke defiantly went on air to deny the child abuse claims which were being made against him. In the recording from 1978, he told Radio Dublin listeners: "How does one disprove such an allegation that children were allowed into Radio Dublin and were molested? Yes, they were the allegations laid down against me." He went on: "All I could do was deny it and ask for proof." Despite questions being raised over his erratic behaviour as well as the child abuse claims being made against him in 1978, Radio Dublin lasted into the late '90s with the pervert at its helm.

Cooke didn't have any friends, he couldn't relate to adults, according to many of those who knew him. Instead, he surrounded himself with children who he was able to easily control and manipulate. He liked being in charge and got a kick out of dominating youngsters, one of his many victims said. According to Siobhan, whose initial claims in 1978 resulted in many of the DJs leaving the station, Cooke was able to hide in plain sight while continuing to abuse children. She suffered horrific abuse at the hands of the well-known broadcaster, the effects of which have stayed with her until this day.

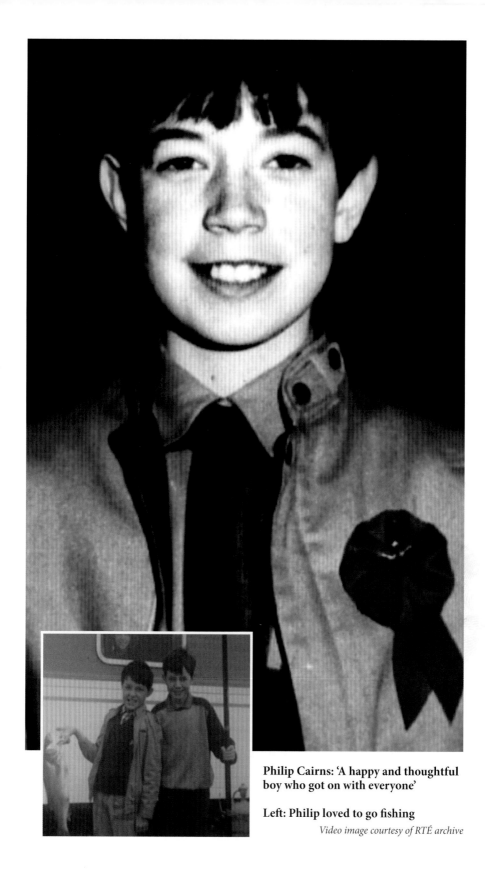

**Philip Cairns: 'A happy and thoughtful boy who got on with everyone'**

**Left: Philip loved to go fishing**

*Video image courtesy of RTÉ archive*

**All together for Philip: Local people were quick to respond to an appeal for help, hundreds rallying to search the surrounding area in October 1986** *Video images courtesy of RTÉ archive*

**Sinister discovery: Philip's bag was found in a local laneway – the only evidence in the case**

**Heartbreak: The pain is clear to see as Philip's mother Alice and father Philip face the press.**
**Below: Gardai quiz motorists on the busy Ballyroan Road** *Video images courtesy of RTÉ archive*

HAVE YOU SEEN THIS BOY ?

Phone : 931211

**Portraits of a monster: (Above) images of prime suspect Eamon Cooke**

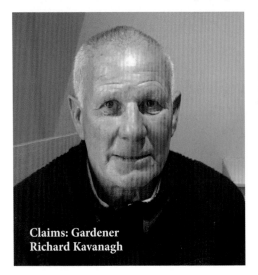

**Claims: Gardener
Richard Kavanagh**

**Suffering: Ann Boyle (above) in 2007,
holding a picture of her three children.
Mary is wearing the red top and her
sister Ann is on the right**

**Brave: Daughter Nikita Cooke (left) had the courage to confront her father (above) and ask him questions that had always played on her mind**

*Image left courtesy of Martin Doran Photography*

Crime scene: Another search for Philip in later years – at The Grange Golf Club in Rathfarnham in 2009. Advances in science could yet hold the key to the case

Ongoing investigation: Mother Alice and father Philip access an official database in 2004

Still searching: Sisters Suzanne and Sandra Cairns at the launch of the new missing children's website at Garda headquarters in Phoenix Park in 2004

Theories: Dr Julian Boon (top) and Professor John O'Keefe. (Right) former Detective Sergeant Tom Doyle back at the scene of the laneway. He has never given up hope

Boy to man: An age-progressed image of Philip as a 21-year-old

'I believe there are people who may have information': Superintendent Peter Duff (left) makes a renewed appeal in 2016

Tree of hope: Minister for Justice, Equality and Defence, Alan Shatter TD and Philip's mum Alice on Ireland's inaugural Missing Persons Day in 2013

'If only that schoolbag could talk'… deeper DNA investigation could yet provide vital information to solve the mystery and bring some closure to the family

*Video image courtesy of RTÉ archive*

As a young child, Siobhan lived just doors away from the studio and would spend her days playing in and around the house Cooke owned. The pervert groomed her from the age of seven over the course of three years, with the level of abuse gradually progressing and getting worse as time went on. Siobhan said Cooke took his time grooming her, so that her young innocent mind wouldn't question a sudden change in his behaviour towards her.

"It was a very slow gradual process. He would say, 'Oh, I have puppies in the garden,' and we would go down and play with them and then it was, 'Oh, you can come into the house and have a look around'. He had a grand piano we could play and he had a phone and he would let us ring up people, stupid little things really. Then he would say, 'Oh, don't tell your mammy or daddy or you won't be allowed to be here again'. As time went on, the level of abuse intensified. Then he introduced touching and he would give you 50 pence or 20 pence and that was a lot of money. I do remember, when it progressed into the bedroom, he would say, 'Ah, jump on the bed, take your clothes off there,' and then he would bring in the touching part. I remember thinking, 'This doesn't feel right, this is a bit strange'."

The horrible stench of body odour and cigarette smoke from him was nauseating, Siobhan recalled. "He was absolutely filthy. If I go into a supermarket now and I see a man with a black grease mark around the neck of his shirt I have to walk out. The smell of cigarettes off him was disgusting. He was always stinking and he was my introduction to body odour. I had a father and he never smelt like that. Cooke was always oily from tinkering with cars too."

It would be years before Cooke would face charges for the horrific abuse he inflicted on Siobhan. In March 2007 he was convicted of 42 counts of indecent assault against two young girls, one being Siobhan, between the years 1976 and 1978. The case, which ran for 16 days at the Central Criminal Court, heard how his victims had named him "the Cookie monster". Ms Justice Maureen Clark told Siobhan and the other female victim: "It has been a long five or six years for all of you and maybe a lifetime for some. I hope today gives you some sense of finality and you never have to appear in court again." She sentenced Cooke to 10 years in prison comprising one year from each of the 42 counts, with five years to run consecutively for each of the two victims and the remaining 32 terms to run concurrently.

The court heard from Inspector Gerard Kelly how Cooke had been convicted after a trial in 2003 and sentenced to 10 years for attempted rape, attempted unlawful carnal knowledge and sexual and indecent assault of four girls, including the two complainants in the current case. However, following a legal technicality, this conviction was subsequently quashed and he was released in May 2006. Inspector Kelly told the court Cooke had eight previous convictions spanning 51 years. They included shooting with intent, arson, malicious damage and contempt of court. The father of 11 denied all charges at the time and claimed the allegations were made to "blacken my name" and to divert attention away from an employee he said he fired for "embezzling money from the company".

Siobhan decided at the time to bravely waive her anonymity in order to tell the world of her horrific ordeal in the hope that other people in similar situations would find the strength to seek help. And she said even at the court case as an adult, Cooke tried to intimidate her. "In court I had my husband on one side of me and Cooke sat down on the other. He was writing my name down on a piece of paper, over and over again. He tried to intimidate me out of the court. I had to put my hand up, like a child at school, and ask why he was allowed to sit beside me. But I wasn't going through all this for me, because there were a hundred more behind me. I wouldn't be able to even put a number on the amount of victims there are for Eamon Cooke. I'm not talking 10 or 20 or even 30, I know of at least 20 and there are so many more who have never come forward. There are so many more out there who have never come forward out of absolute fear, so many. The only thing is that now he's dead, other people might decide to come forward too."

Siobhan said the manipulative molester became close friends with people who were pillars of society and deemed by the community to be powerful, influential and in many respects untouchable. She believes this was as a means of protection, a way of stopping people from getting too close to finding out the truth about his sickening crimes.

Despite not being religious, Cooke knew priests and Siobhan said she recalled one in particular that the abuser knew well. She said Cooke and Fr Michael Cleary, who had a long relationship with his housekeeper with whom he fathered two sons, were good friends. In fact, Cleary even had his own show on the station. Cleary was loved and respected and for Cooke that was the perfect cover, according to Siobhan.

At the time, Cleary was sharing a house with notorious child abuser Fr Tony Walsh from Ballyfermot, who was known as 'the singing priest' and would later be charged for indecently assaulting a number of young boys and girls. He had carried out sickening crimes against his victims, including raping a young boy with a crucifix. In fact, when the mother of one young boy accused Walsh of abusing her son, Cleary – who was also a curate in Ballyfermot, Dublin, at the time – he went to the boy's house to speak to him to "educate him on issues of male sexuality" and left. Siobhan recalls Walsh and Cleary sharing a parish house at one point and how on one occasion, when in the presence of rapist Walsh, he began massaging her shoulders and she remembers how uncomfortable it made her feel. She said Cooke wasn't there at the time but pointed out how it was extraordinary that two prolific paedophiles lived and abused in such close proximity to one another, one based in Inchicore and the other in Ballyfermot, only a few kilometres away.

There were a number of paedophiles living and abusing within the small Dublin suburban area. Fr Bill Carney, who also spent his formative years in Ballyfermot, was a rampant child abuser who terrorised and destroyed many lives. He died in 2015 at the age of 65, while in prison on remand awaiting trial on 34 historic charges of sexually abusing eight boys and two girls over a 20-year period up to 1989. Carney, who was dismissed from the clerical state in 1992 following almost a decade of abuse complaints, was regarded as one of the most notorious cleric sex abusers of his generation. Like fellow paedophile Cooke, he was obnoxious towards those who got in his way. He used his position of power to get close to children in residential care and swimming classes. Did all the local paedophile priests and Cooke know of one another and their sickening sadistic crimes or was it just coincidental?

In May 2009, Judge Yvonne Murphy said in her three-volume report on clerical sex abuse in the Dublin archdiocese that she found some "worrying connections" between some paedophile priests but said there was no evidence to suggest they were part of a "paedophile ring."

The Murphy Commission of Inquiry identified 320 people who had complained of child sexual abuse between 1975 and 2004. The report detailed the cases of 46 priests who were guilty of abuse as a representative sample of the 102 priests within its remit. One priest alone admitted to abusing more than 100 children while another admitted committing abuse every two weeks for more than 25 years. At the time, the then Garda Commissioner, Fachtna Murphy, said the report made for "difficult and disturbing reading, detailing may instances of sexual abuse and failure to protect victims."

Although he was friends with a number of priests, many of whom it would later emerge were paedophiles, Cooke himself had the audacity to write a letter to the *Irish Independent* complaining about members of the clergy who had been convicted of such horrific crimes.

In the Letters To The Editor section of the paper in October 1995 which I tracked down, a few years before he would himself be charged for his own sickening abuse, he wrote: "Sir – Having followed the clerical abuse scandal for the past year, I would like to make some observations on the Church handling of many cases. We have heard statements from Bishop McKiernan, the man who knew 20 years ago of Fr Brendan Smyth's abuse of children. A man who could have stopped untold suffering by so many children. 'I acted honourably. My conscience is clear'. Insists he made no attempt to cover up the Smyth case.

'I had to follow the rules. The only action I could take was to stop Fr Smyth hearing confession'. Is this a joke? No. This was Bishop McKiernan talking to a newspaper reporter. If this is punishment to fit the crime I can see how seriously the Church views sexual abuse of children. Take 50 lines, my son. With all the recent assurances given by the Church we still see attempts to stifle publicity." Later in the letter he went on: "These are the people who failed to report the criminal activities of so many of their clergy. Blatant hypocrisy. Is it any wonder so many disillusioned people now seek consolation in other religions. My simple message to the hierarchy is practise what you preach – charity and compassion. Report all suspicions of child abuse. Seek financial help from your parishioners if necessary – many are only too willing to help. Eamon Cooke, Wheatfield Court, Clondalkin, Dublin 22."

As well as abusing numerous children over the years, Cooke also had a long history of violence.

From an early age he was getting into trouble with the law. At just 12 he was arrested and charged £40 for blowing up the O'Connell Monument in Glasnevin Cemetery. He boastfully wrote years later: "At around 12 I got to making what would today be called a pipe bomb. A few of us decided that we would put it in the top of the O'Connell Monument in Glasnevin Cemetery, so one night I climbed over the gate and made my way up to the top, lit a candle fuse and we all went back home to watch the light flickering in the window. We were talking about it outside a neighbour's house and she rang the gardaí. The bomb blew up and I was arrested and fined £40 for the damages to the windows. I told my father all about it. I said

I had no problem in owning up to the damage but I was not willing to involve anyone else."

As a teenager Cooke also gained an interest in the IRA. In 1978, a report in Magill described him as "an innocuous, quietly-spoken IRA man". In his own words, Cooke said he became interested with the terrorist organisation from a young age. "At school I got interested in history, where I had a very republican-minded teacher from Finglas. I became more involved with republicans as time went by and the story to my mother at weekends was that I was gone cycling to An Oige hostel. There was what they called training in the Dublin Mountains, whereas it was really an endurance test of how long one could live in the open with no food and still travel long distances. Then there were the trips up North on what everyone called bombing runs. There was only one IRA at the time, no provos and the word terrorist had not come into use," he wrote.

But his love of the IRA dwindled in the latter part of his life when a number of well-known dissidents took over Radio Dublin. Cooke wrote in 2001 of his anger at what had occurred following the death of Bobby Sands in 1981 and how the violent encounter led him to question their motives and his involvement with the organisation. "After his death, subversives took over a number of illegal radio stations to broadcast propaganda. Twenty of them, well-known republicans, came to our station in Inchicore one Sunday morning in May. I refused to let them in and they simply smashed their way in and wrecked the place when they found all equipment had been switched off. One of my staff got an eye injury from flying glass and I had a fractured arm when hit with a scaffolding pole.

Convoys of armed gardaí arrived and after (named individual) threatened to burn the house down if I did not switch back on the equipment they left. No one was arrested. That ended all my contacts with subversives except for one occasion when I needed help a few years later in Scotland."

In 1957, when working as a clerk, Cooke was also arrested following a shootout with gardaí in Bray, Co Wicklow. On the night of February 18 he had fired six times at Gardaí at a Hollybrook Garage, near Wingfield. He escaped but was arrested the following day by officers. He was charged with the attempted murder of four guards; discharging a loaded revolver at them; with possession of a firearm with intent to endanger life and with malicious damage. In court he stated he had "no intention to endanger life" but said "I admit some damages".

In a statement, Cooke said he had noticed the garage after being in the Dublin Mountains with friends shooting and decided to raid it for petrol. He claimed to have bought the gun, which he had used to fire at officers, six months earlier to shoot at birds. Cooke was sentenced to five years at Wicklow Circuit Court for shooting at officers and firearm possession. According to Cooke he then spent time between two different prisons.

He said in unearthed documents: "Around 1955, there was a petrol strike. People had organised a trip northwards and with the lack of petrol three of us decided to acquire some from a closed garage in Bray. I then had a driving licence so I hired a car, we loaded two drums on board and set off for Bray. Since we planned to head to a meeting with others in Drogheda we were armed. Gardaí arrived on the scene, we fired shots in the air and escaped on foot." But he said the law caught up with him the next morning. "The next morning I arrived home and was arrested. My dad got me a solicitor who wanted me to plead not guilty to everything. He said I could get a long sentence if I did not and refused to name the others with me. I pleaded guilty and was sentenced to five years for the possession of firearms. A few weeks of this was spent in Mountjoy and the remainder in Portlaoise."

There are also doubts hanging over the cause of his first wife's death. Helena Cooke, who Cooke called Lena, dropped dead suddenly at the age of 27 on April 3, 1965, from a suspected heart attack. The couple had met in 1960 and a year later were married.

Following her sudden death Cooke claimed he slept every night for two months at her graveside in Glasnevin cemetery before receiving her insurance money and fleeing on a motorbike to Austria. Describing her health years later, Cooke would write: "Lena had a murmur on her heart from birth but it was never a problem. She wanted children and try as we did, it never came about." He went on: "Then on the 3rd of April 1965 Lena got up apparently to make a cup of tea at around five in the morning and dropped dead from a heart attack. I heard the noise of her falling and went downstairs, carried her to bed and rang an ambulance. I woke the girl next door, who was a nurse, but nothing could be done."

Lena Cooke's death certificate has been reported to state she died from ventricular fibrillation and acute myocardial failure. Both conditions are also caused by electrocution. Professor Mike Morse, of the University of San Diego, told a newspaper in December 2016 that her cause of death would perhaps be worth investigating further. Prof Morse said at the time: "Generally, electrically-induced ventricular fibrillation shows no evidence on autopsy with the exception of entry or exit burns or marking. Given the low probability of fibrillation in a 27-year-old with no observable heart defect, this is a suspicious mystery. The fact she is an electrician's wife should have caused the coroner to want to look deeper for earmarks of electrical injury."

Although nobody suspected anything untoward at the time, a former partner of Cooke has told me how she now believes he may have killed Lena and former detectives who met him over the years are now also of the belief that her death should be re-examined. Did the qualified electrician have a role to play in her death or did she die from a heart attack as he stated?

His former wife recalled to me how Cooke often physically abused her and therefore was more than capable of doing the same to his first wife. She also claims that Cooke once told her Lena had died after falling down the stairs and said it was suspicious as he once kicked her down a fleet of stairs during their violent and volatile relationship.

Speaking about her time with Cooke, his former partner told me of the horrendous abuse she suffered at his hands. "He thought he was above the law. Life with Cooke when I first met him was OK. I married him within six weeks of meeting him. I guess the thought of someone loving me made me fall for him, I was very young at the time. I ran to a police station one night after being beat up by him, they rang him and said "bring your wife home". Things were different then for victims of domestic violence. There was no help. Cooke told me that his first wife Lena died, she fell down the stairs. I was kicked down the stairs by Cooke. He once told a social worker he would blow her head off too."

Former Garda Cold Case Detective Alan Bailey, who met Cooke over the years while on duty, believes Lena's cause of death should be reinvestigated. "I would suggest that the circumstances surrounding the death of his wife be revisited with a view to establishing if the investigation should be reopened in light of what we now know about him."

Bailey said he first came across Cooke, who he described as a horrible, creepy individual, at a crime scene. He said that, along with other officers, he quickly got frustrated with him arriving there before they had. Cooke would listen in on the garda frequency and then race the other squad cars to get there first. "I first came into contact with Cooke back in the Seventies. He was kind of a police groupie, he turned up at every crime scene. Often, you would find with him that you were beaten to the scene by him. And the more gruesome the scene, the better the chance you had of finding him at it."

The former detective said there was one particularly gruesome incident which Cooke turned up at which sticks in his mind to this day. "There was a murder on the grounds of St Brendan's Hospital in Dublin, way back in the late Seventies, early Eighties, and when we arrived at the scene he was at it already. We got a call to attend with the ambulance and his standard excuse at the time was that he was there because he was a member of the media. He was absolutely sleazy. He was hanging on the periphery of all these crime scenes and would have been in the middle of them if given half the chance."

Bailey said he was not surprised when Cooke's name was suggested in regards to Philip's disappearance. He said despite initially thinking he was only interested in abusing young girls, he now believes Cooke was capable of anything. "I was only surprised that I felt his victims were female rather than male. But then again, nothing shocks me. It would certainly be in him."

Journalist Paul Williams, who wrote about Cooke over the years and even once met up with the paedophile to interview him while he was on the run from gardaí, said the child abuser was one of the most evil individuals he had ever met during the course of his long career. "He really was a Pied Piper-type character, kind of like the Jimmy Savile of Irish radio. He was a complete sleazebag. If there was ever someone wearing a sign with 'paedo' written on it, it was him. Everything about him was just wrong. He was a small, dirty, really repulsive individual. He had disgustingly dirty hands, I will never forget them. His nails were all filthy."

Williams, who was working with the *Sunday World* newspaper at the time, recalled meeting the DJ while he was wanted by gardaí in 2002. The pair had arranged to meet at the Red Cow Hotel in Dublin following a number of exchanges. "At the time he was wanted by the gardaí. He also produced an old photograph to show me of a woman with her top off.

"I have met a lot of paedophiles and all kinds of strange people throughout my life but he really was one of the worst. He was a manipulator and a typical paedophile. He was very good, a class master at manipulation and particularly with people weaker than himself.

"He was good at exploiting people's weaknesses, particularly young people. There was a vibe that just came off him, which was hard to put your finger on, which was just so repulsive.

This guy, no matter how hard he tried, could not disguise what he was."

And in a letter shown to me by Williams which had been penned by Cooke, the paedophile even called out the way in which children were being treated while in state care, claiming they were both physically and sexually abused.

In the typed letter from October 2, 2002, Cooke wrote: "Does anyone, including yourself, understand or even care what happens to children in care? Places like Artane, Letterfrack, St Joseph's in Kilkenny, Goldenbridge Convent, the Magdalene Laundries are no longer new. We are told these things which happened in these places will never happen again, as if someone just waved a magic wand and it stopped. Children are still abused and molested."

Williams recalled how he tipped the guards off about Cooke's whereabouts following their secret rendezvous at the Red Cow in Dublin. "When I met him, he was on the run. I rang the guards and said: 'Look I'm going to be meeting him, here he is, come and take him'. And that's how he ended up getting arrested."

But when asked if he personally believed Cooke had any role to play in Philip's disappearance and alleged murder, Williams said he was not so sure. "I did bits and pieces on the Philip Cairns case, it happened just before I came to Dublin. I couldn't say if Cooke was a murderer or not. But if there was such a thing as a stereotypical paedophile, he was certainly that."

While Cooke was serving his sentence for child abuse at Dublin's Arbour Hill Prison, an advocate for abuse victims, Angela Copley, came forward saying she had approached the gardaí after hearing of claims through a third party that Cooke was behind the abduction and murder of young schoolboy Philip Cairns in 1986. Ms Copley, who has sadly passed away since, had heard how a woman, who was abused by Cooke as a child, had alleged that he had hit the teenager over the head at his Radio Dublin studio.

Since the shocking revelation in 2016, many have speculated as to who the woman in question might be, with some believing it to be his victim Siobhan Kennedy-McGuinness. However, the now 53-year-old told me that it was not her who witnessed the incident, although she believes she knows who the woman in question is.

Cooke's victim, who was nine at the time of Philip's disappearance, told detectives that on the day the teenager went missing she was in a car with Cooke. She said the DJ had promised the youngster a tour of the radio studio and while showing him around, a row broke out between the two. She claims she was in another room at the time but managed to witness Cooke striking the young boy with an implement over the head and saw him lying on the floor unconscious. She allegedly told officers how she ran for the front door but Cooke caught up with her and how she had no recollection of what happened after that.

The woman's claims, which were described at the time and since as being very credible, were only followed up by officers in 2016 despite the woman first contacting gardaí years earlier. It was reported that she initially came forward following an appeal into the case in 2011 but refused to give a statement at the time. She was allegedly terrified of Cooke, which accounted for her initial trepidation. But five years later, after learning he was on his deathbed and no longer posed a threat, it's understood she decided to give the guards the signed statement they required as she deemed it safe to do so.

The signed statement meant the guards could now officially go and quiz the paedophile. One detective, who reflected the same statement as many others I have talked to, said: "What you have to remember is that Cooke absolutely terrified people and had a history of violence towards those who crossed him. This woman was a victim of Cooke's and had endured years of abuse at his hands. People were very quick to judge her waiting to come forward but for her it was an extremely hard thing to do. This monster had such a grip over those he abused that even in old age they feared him. Her bravery to finally come forward should be commended. People sitting and typing nasty things about her on social media need to put their feet in her shoes for a moment and realise how hard it was for her."

Despite Cooke only being interviewed in 2016 by detectives, officers had been looking to see if there was a possible connection between him and Philip's disappearance as far back as 2008. Despite them not being able to connect him to the case, he was known to authorities for abusing children and there was also circumstantial evidence which led officers to take a closer look at him. It included him having access to a red car which fitted the same description as one reported to officers by a local Rathfarnham man who claims he spotted a boy who looked like Philip on the day of his disappearance talking to a person in a similar vehicle.

Siobhan believes she knows the woman in question who made the claims against the paedophile and said, if it is in fact her, she would believe the information to be extremely credible. She is also of the belief that he often drugged his victims. "I have met this woman, I have spent time with her. The reason in my estimation as to why she came forward when she did was because she believed she was safe and he couldn't touch her. There is no reason why that girl would walk in and say what she did unless it was true. I would put my life on it. There is no reason in my mind as to why she would do that."

And Siobhan said there might be a possibility that the girl couldn't remember what happened following Cooke assaulting Philip as she may have been drugged. "That girl in her statement allegedly said she remembered Philip getting a slap or he fell and that she thinks she was drugged because she just woke up. I believe I was drugged by him as a child, too.

"There was one occasion that I believe he definitely drugged me as I woke up in his bed very disoriented after receiving some fruit and jellies from him."

She believes if Cooke had a part to play in the schoolboy's abduction he wouldn't have been able to hide it. "If they had only got to him sooner. He loved his own ego. He wouldn't have admitted it but he would have tripped up and let something slip."

Officers decided to go and interview Cooke at Dublin's Arbour Hill Prison. Detectives would quickly discover Cooke was no longer locked up in the jail alongside other well-known child abusers, including Patrick O'Brien and double killer John Shaw, but was in fact at St Francis Hospice in Raheny, Dublin.

They were extremely disheartened to learn, however, just how sick the pervert was and how little time they would have to quiz him. With his declining health, detectives working on the case only had days to try to obtain the information needed.

Rarely seen without a cigarette in his hand, Cooke had been diagnosed with terminal lung cancer and was dying. At the age of 79, the years of heavy smoking had finally caught up with him. Detectives were now in a race against time to try to establish if the 'Cookie Monster', as he was known to his many victims, was in fact involved in Philip's disappearance.

The prisoner, who had been treated like a celebrity by fellow inmates up until his transfer to the hospice, was now on a lot of medication and drifted in and out of consciousness. He also had a chesty cough and at times struggled to catch his breath.

Officers interviewed him twice while at the hospice but only managed to get 'yes' and 'no' answers out of him mostly but they were confident that some of the information given to them by the witness was credible. He is understood to have admitted knowing Philip but offered no further information as to what happened on the day in question nor gave any indication as to where his body might be buried.

It's believed officers pleaded with him to confess before he died but he stayed tight-lipped. The paedophile, even at death's door, would not give detectives the answers they desperately needed to finally solve the case. He died leaving more questions than answers as to whether in fact he was involved in Philip's disappearance. Not even with just days to live could the child abuser reveal either way if he had a role to play in the teenager's abduction, giving the Cairns family some form of closure after so many years. It would be the closest detectives would get to making an arrest in the case.

# 9.

# Victims

*'You have memorials but it's not the same. You just want to know where they are. It's the not knowing which is torture. Mary is always on my mind. I think about her every day'*

There have been many high-profile missing children cases internationally. Perhaps the most well-known of them all is that of Madeleine McCann, who is believed to have been snatched from her family's holiday apartment in Portugal on May 3, 2007.

The English toddler's parents had been having dinner with friends in the complex restaurant 100 yards away when her mother, Kate, returned to check up on the three-year-old and her twin brother and sister, only to discover she was gone. After realising her daughter was no longer in her bed, panic set in instantly and the police were called and a full-scale search of the Ocean Club as well as the surrounding area of Praia da Luz was carried out.

On May 12, the Portuguese police said they believed that Madeleine had been abducted but was still alive and in Portugal. Later that month they issued a description of a man who was allegedly seen carrying a young child fitting the little girl's description close to the holiday complex roughly around the time she is believed to have been snatched. Despite claims of various sightings of the little blonde-haired girl with two distinctive different coloured eyes, Madeleine, who would now be a teenager, has never been found.

The most recent and promising breakthrough in the case came in June 2020 when police officers revealed that a 43-year-old German prisoner, who was referred to in German media as Christian B, was identified as a possible suspect. He was allegedly living in the area at the time of her disappearance, and managed to live under the radar of local authorities. Gerry and Kate McCann said at the time of the development that they were still hopeful of finding their little girl alive. "All we have ever wanted is to find her, uncover the truth and bring those responsible to justice. We will never give up hope of finding Madeleine alive, but whatever the outcome may be, we need to know as we need to find peace."

Before Madeleine's high-profile abduction there was another case which grabbed the world's attention in a similar way. It involved six-year-old American boy Etan Patz, who disappeared in New York on May 25, 1979, while en route to his school bus stop two blocks away in the Soho neighbourhood of Lower Manhattan. He became one of the first missing children in the

US to ever have his photograph placed on the side of a milk carton in the form of state-wide appeal.

Like in the Philip Cairns case, many years passed without any breakthroughs in the investigation but his heartbroken parents, like the Irish teenager's, never gave up searching for their little boy. It was only in 2012, 33 years later, when a man contacted officers to share his suspicions about his brother-in-law possibly being involved in the case that developments in the investigation were quickly made. It would emerge that Pedro Hernandez, who was an 18-year-old stock boy at a Soho deli at the time of the disappearance, had kidnapped and murdered the youngster. He confessed to the horrendous crime but unfortunately the little boy's remains have never been found.

Across the world there are many missing children cases. In the United States alone, the FBI estimates that 800,000 kids go missing nationwide each year on average. In England, an estimated 112,853 juveniles are reported missing annually. While most cases transpire to be relatively straightforward and resolved within a matter of days, sometimes, very rarely in fact, it transpires that there is a far more sinister motive behind it. Over the years there have been a handful of prominent cases of young children being snatched off the streets and held captive against their will for months and, in some cases, years.

Some of the most shocking cases have occurred stateside in recent years. One of the most horrifying incidents in America involved a 14-year-old girl by the name of Elizabeth Smart who was kidnapped by deranged couple Brian David Mitchell and his wife Wanda Barzee on June 5, 2002, and held hostage for nine months.

Then there was the case of seven-year-old Jaycee Dugard,

who was kidnapped by Phillip Garrido with the help of his wife, Nancy, on June 10, 1991 in Meyers, California, and held captive for a staggering 18 years before being rescued. There have been no such cases in Ireland to date, or at least none which have come to light and been reported. There is the possibility this could be the case with Philip but to many, including officers who have worked on the investigation, it's highly unlikely.

The most up-to-date figures for Irish missing children cases were published by An Garda Siochana for the months of January to September 2020. They showed that there were a total of 4,627 people under the age of 18 who were reported to authorities, with 4,609 later being found. The incredibly low figure further highlights that the number of children who go missing in Ireland never to be seen again as extremely rare.

For the families of those who simply disappear without a trace there is one thing worse than finding a body and that's not finding one. For the majority of those who I have spoken to, it's not knowing what happened to their loved one which causes the most pain. They spend months and years questioning whether they are in fact still alive or if they died and are yet to be found.

There have only ever been two highly publicised cases similar to Philip's over the last 50 years which have pulled at the heartstrings of the nation as much.

One such case involved six-year-old Mary Boyle, who vanished while at her grandparents' small dairy farm in Cashelard, Co Donegal, on March 18, 1977. Like with Philip's case, the young girl's disappearance from the remote and boggy townland outside Ballyshannon has never been solved and her family have continued to try to establish what happened to her. The 3ft 11in tall girl's disappearance and lack of evidence surrounding the case has baffled investigating officers ever since. Her case is the longest running high-profile unsolved missing child case in the country. Like with the schoolboy's investigation, Mary is presumed dead by her loved ones despite her body never being found and still being categorised as a missing person case.

The bubbly and outgoing little girl, wearing a lilac knitted jumper, had been playing outside when she decided to follow her uncle Gerry Gallagher, who was dropping back a ladder he had borrowed from neighbour Patrick McCawley. Her small legs weren't able for the task at hand and she decided to give up halfway across the 450-yard boggy strip of land, weighed down by her Wellington boots, and turned back to return home. It would be the last time the blonde-haired little girl, who was last seen eating a bag of sweets, would be seen alive. Mary, who was always spotted with a smile on her face, literally vanished, never to be seen again. No evidence was ever discovered and her remains were never found.

One of the most frustrating aspects of the case is that there was no evidence found; no garments of clothing to retrieve DNA samples from or footprints to cross-reference. A fingertip search of all nearby land, as well as a lake, were also carried out but turned up nothing. Her heartbroken parents Ann and Charlie Boyle, twin sister Ann and older brother Patrick have tirelessly searched for her over the years ever since, never giving up hope of one day finding the once happy little girl. Was she abducted that Friday afternoon or did a desolate patch of marshy land swallow her up? This latter theory is unlikely, though there were a number of marshland areas searched at the time. It's highly believed by all involved that something far more sinister happened to the girl.

In 2011, a second review of the case was undertaken by An Garda Siochana's Northern Region. Like with Philip's case, the gardaí also released an image of what they believed Mary would look like at her current age. Being an identical twin, it was easy to configure an image of the bubbly youngster as a young woman.

Three years later, officers re-examining the case arrested a man in connection to Mary's disappearance. At the time her mother Ann said she didn't recognise the man who gardaí had taken into custody but said he was "from the general area". The convicted sex offender, who was 64 in 2014, was quizzed following the breakthrough in the case. He was serving a sentence at the time at the Midlands Prison in Portlaoise, Co Laois, for the sexual abuse of two boys in the Sixties and Seventies.

The Assistant Commissioner for the Northern Region at the time, Kieran Kenny, said the arrest was made following new evidence obtained by the Review Team which had been set up in 2011. "A dedicated team of personnel have been working on this investigation which has involved the pursuit of new lines of enquiry, a review of material already available and also involved extensive searches with the benefit of forensic and geology experts." But despite the breakthrough in the case, the man was later released without charge.

Speaking about the man in question at the time, Mrs Boyle said he was someone who she had heard of before but didn't personally know. "This person wouldn't have been known to

Mary because Mary lived in Kincasslagh. I would have slightly known him I think. I have heard of him before but that is it. The Garda have never given up on Mary and the Garda have always contacted me and let me know what's happening in Mary's case. If he did do something on Mary let the Garda know and tell them where she is," the widow told the *Irish Daily Mirror* at the time.

Notorious Scottish child killer Robert Black was another sexual predator who had been previously linked with Mary's disappearance as he was working in the area at the time. However, the link could never be stood up. The former delivery driver murdered four schoolgirls between 1981 and 1986. In May 1994, he was convicted of kidnapping, raping and murdering three of his victims. Police established that Black regularly travelled to Northern Ireland and the Republic as part of his work. In fact, at one stage it was even suggested that he was going to be quizzed over the Philip Cairns case too but nothing further ever emerged from the claims.

In 2016, a fisherman by the name of PJ Coughlan came forward claiming to have seen a red Volkswagen Beetle speeding away from the area where the little girl had disappeared. He said he saw the girl being driven away in a car 10 minutes before he witnessed Mary's uncle Gerry frantically looking for her. He said at the time: "I believe I saw her being driven away in a car. There's no doubt in my mind she was lifted."

Mary's twin sister, Ann Doherty, who has never given up trying to find out what happened to her that fateful day, said her sibling's disappearance has never left her and there is not a day that goes by that she doesn't think about her. Speaking from her home in Donegal, Ann told me that she remembers the day her sister was taken despite being young at the time. "I would have a strong enough recollection of that day, it completely changed me. Silly little things like being scared that someone was going to come for me too. My whole life changed because I had to face everything on my own.

"Up until then, I always had someone by my side. We were really close and would have done everything together. Mary was the chatty one and I was the quiet one. She was more feisty and would stand up to people whereas I wouldn't have."

She has her suspicions as to who took her sister that day in 1977. "I have a fair idea of who I think it is. If somebody comes forward with a better explanation I will listen to them but at the moment I can't find one. I would sit and listen to anyone. It's very very frustrating that we can't seem to get anywhere."

Not a day goes by that Ann doesn't think about her sister and all the key moments in life that they should have been enjoying together. She said life had been extremely tough for her not having her by her side. "I have gone through a lot of milestones without Mary. They have had a huge impact on me because you have to face them on your own. I have had to make my communion, my confirmation, getting married, having kids – everything Mary should have been there to celebrate too. My 50th birthday was a very hard day. I know everyone was doing their best to enjoy it but it was a hard day, she should have been there too. It's had a huge impact on me. It does make you question people too, you certainly wouldn't be as trusting as what maybe you should be."

The family are not out for revenge or to lock up Mary's abductor, they just want to know where her remains are so they can give her a proper burial and have a grave to visit. "I know it would be hard to have a grave but at least we would have somewhere to go and talk to Mary. You have memorials and things like that but it's just not the same, you just want to know where they are. It's the not knowing which is torture. Mary is always on my mind. I think about her every day."

But Mary's heartbroken sister said she believes someone out there knows what happened to her and is appealing for them to find it in their heart and conscience to come forward. "I'm asking anyone who has information, as little as they might know, to come forward. No matter how little they know it could just be the clue that we need to find Mary, the final piece of the jigsaw that you need. Any bit of information, please come forward. What would they do if it was one of their own? They would want answers. It is never too late. We are not interested in anyone going to jail, we just want to bury Mary. It's not about justice, it's about finding Mary and putting her in a grave, in consecrated ground, just to know where she is. It's not about chasing anyone down." Gerry Gallagher, Mary's uncle, is the last person known to have seen her. Is there someone out there who spotted the little girl after that? All known potential suspects, perverts or sexual offenders were all checked and ruled out.

Another major case which made national headlines at the time was the abduction, rape and murder of little Bernadette Connolly in Sligo. The 10-year-old was reported missing at 4.30pm on April 17, 1970, after disappearing while en route to a friend's house two-and-a-half miles away in the remote area of Collooney. The family had spent close to three years in the area after moving home from Birmingham in England as they believed it would be a safer place to rear a young family. Bernadette, or Bernie as she was known to her family and friends, was sent by her mother Maureen to collect some smoked haddock and potatoes from family friend Eileen Molloy in Lissaneena. The brown-eyed girl, with red hair and freckles, shouted out "bye mom" as she set off on her short journey.

Heading in the direction of Cloonamahon, she cycled past Kathleen Flynn and her 12-year-old son, Oliver, who were delivering coal by horse and cart. It would be the last time the little girl would be seen alive – she never arrived at the Molloys' house. Somewhere along the way she was abducted and killed. There is no way of knowing what route Bernadette took that day once she got as far as the Cloonamahon Monastery, whether she cut through the grounds of the religious retreat itself or proceeded along what was known locally as 'the lake road', which ran beside it.

When Bernadette had not arrived home as expected by 6pm, her mother sent her older sister, Ann, to go and find her. But when her concerned sibling made it to the Molloys' home she was told that her sister had never arrived that afternoon. Fear set in and, with the news she had just been told, Ann began to panic. So along with one of the Molloy daughters, Patricia, the pair frantically set off in a bid to retrace Bernadette's steps and hopefully find her. As they made their way back to the family house, they discovered her bicycle and her mother's purse, still containing 10 shillings and two pence, in an embankment close to the monastery. A footprint, which was believed to be that of a man, was also found on the ground close by.

The pair instantly knew something was wrong and Ann raced back to tell her parents about their chilling discovery.

Straight away her mother started to ring around the local hospitals and doctors to see if they had Bernadette in their care while her father Gerry went back to where the bike had been found. There, he was met by local officers who had been called.

Speaking about the day, Bernadette's sister recounted how the events unfolded. "As a rule I was always sent for messages but I hadn't been home from school. A neighbour had rang and asked did we want to collect something from the shop and that she would bring it over for us. But when Bernie was at home, mam sent her. We were always warned in England at the time not to talk to strangers. We were aware what could happen. Mam and Dad brought us home because Ireland was their home and you could rear children in comfort, where you wouldn't be hiding them from this sort of thing."

She said she stumbled across her sister's Raleigh Astronaut bike, which was her pride and joy, and her mother's purse by accident. She had initially seen something which caught her eye en route to her neighbour's house but thought nothing of it as they believed the little girl had made it safely to her destination. "For some reason I looked back and thought I saw something shining in the bushes where there was a high ditch." She added: "We went back to the house and alerted Mam and straight away Mam said 'something's happened'. Bernie was shy. If it was me, I would go into a neighbour's house and start chatting. Bernie was so shy she wouldn't get into a car and leave her new bike unless she was forced. Or unless someone in authority told her."

A local farmer had spent the day moving hay from his farm and had seen nothing. Ann said. "He was going up and down the road all day and he saw nothing. There were people working up in the fields, they saw nothing. No one saw anything. Someone must have seen something but they said they saw nothing. And no one came forward. We had no evidence. It was a quiet road but you would hear a car go past if you were working in a field. You are talking about different times. People didn't want to get involved, maybe they didn't trust themselves when they saw what they thought they saw," she told the Sligo Champion years later.

After it was discovered that Bernadette had disappeared, a huge search operation was launched immediately and over 200 officers and civilians searched a 15-square mile area of woodland, fields and bog around Collooney in the hope of locating the little girl. A cast of the footprints found by the bike were also taken and the little girl's prized possession was also taken as evidence for fingerprints.

A day after Bernadette disappeared, gardaí were very clear in their statement that they believed something sinister had happened to her little girl. "We definitely suspect foul play. We are treating this very seriously indeed. We are not confining our search to any particular area but are searching everywhere we might get results. However, the main search in the 15-mile area is around Collooney and Doorla."

Hundreds of fingerprints were taken from all males over the age of 15 living close by and gardaí carried out house-to-house enquiries. Tracker dogs were brought from Dublin to help in the search of the accomplished Irish dancer and every field, ditch and pond were forensically searched.

Chief Superintendent J. Sheehan from Sligo appealed to anyone with information to come forward. "We really have no clues at all. What we must look for now is a body," he said at the time.

Maureen, Bernadette's devastated mother, was inconsolable and had to be sedated as she struggled to deal with the heart wrenching news of her daughter's disappearance. After the young girl was reported missing, Father Columba Kelly from the local monastery moved into the Connolly family home to offer support and help.

Speaking about the decision by Fr Columba, Bernadette's sister Ann said years later that he stayed for a long time with the family. "Even when everyone else was gone, he stayed in our tiny, two-bedroomed house. Looking back now, it seems abnormal that someone would stay on in such a small space for so long. I remember even I thought it was strange, but when I asked about it everyone said, 'It's to support your dad'."

The sisters were members of the youth club run by the monastery for local children so everyone knew Fr Columba. As well as offering to care for the traumatised family, he also looked through and read the sympathy letters which had been sent to them by members of the local community in case someone had decided to send a clue as to the whereabouts of the young girl.

On May 7, 1970, gardaí appealed to the drivers of eight vehicles, which had been seen in the vicinity at the time of the young girl's disappearance, to come forward. They included a large white or light-coloured car, a black Zephyr with a roof rack and a green van. Despite none of the motorists coming forward, gardaí discovered that a green Ford Escort van with a Sligo registration was owned by the nearby Cloonamahon Monastery. When approached about the vehicle's whereabouts on the day of Bernadette's disappearance, nobody could account for its location between the crucial time of 4.30pm and 7.30pm.

Most of the monks and brothers had been watching the Apollo spacecraft splashdown around one TV at the monastery that evening. However, a local garage owner told officers investigating the case that one of the brothers, who we shall call Brother X, had called to the garage that evening to fill the green van up with petrol. When quizzed about this, Brother X denied being at the garage. The claim was refuted around the same time that Father Columba told Bernadette's father Gerry that he had seen a car acting suspiciously outside their home two weeks after she was reported missing.

As the months passed by, Bernadette's family, neighbours and the local tight-knit community secretly prayed for a miracle, that the young girl would be found safe and well. But their hopes were sadly dashed on August 5, 1970, when the 4ft 9in girl's almost completely decomposed remains were discovered by chance on the northern slopes of the Curlew Mountains.

Fragments of a skeleton were found in a drain at the end of a bog five miles north-west of Boyle by Mrs Margaret O'Connor, who had been gathering turf at the time. The rancid smell coming from the drain is what initially made the farmer's wife inspect the area more thoroughly. Mrs O'Connor initially thought that it might have been a decomposed dead sheep but on closer inspection made the grisly discovery.

Officers rushed to the scene where they also located shredded pieces of a brown anorak and a gymslip, the same worn by Bernadette on the day she was reported missing. A number of miraculous medals worn by the religious little girl were also found close by. The drain where Bernadette's remains were discovered led to the bog which was used by local farmers to gather turf. Following the gruesome find, the search for missing Bernadette was upgraded to one of murder and a full-scale manhunt for her killer was launched.

Bernadette's sister, Ann, painfully recalled hearing the harrowing news that her sister's remains had been found. "At that time, Bernie's birthday was on the 1st of August. We always thought that she was alive, but Mom said that on Bernie's birthday, she prayed that we'd find her, dead or alive. She was found a few days later. From what I remember, there was some woman out with her husband in a bog, miles away from any houses, near a bog road. They were collecting turf and she saw something she thought was the body of an animal or something and when they went down they discovered it was a human body. At this stage, I suppose it would be well decayed.

"I never found out what happened to Bernie. When you are the oldest child you more or less look after the younger ones. You keep thinking you should have done something. You think, 'It should have been me who was on that bike'. I was never, ever made to feel guilty about it but when you get older and you think back, you think it should have been me on that bike because it was me every evening," she said in an article in the *Sligo Champion*.

In order to jog people's memory of the day Bernadette went missing, gardaí pointed out that the evening in question was when three American astronauts arrived safely back to Earth after the lunar ship they were on, Apollo 13, had been damaged.

An oxygen tank exploded just 56 hours into the flight and the crew were forced to abort their mission and return to Earth. It was a spectacle which had gripped the entire nation and anyone who was lucky enough to own a television at the time was most likely watching the events as they unfolded.

The young girl's funeral brought hundreds of people to the streets, lining the way for the small white coffin which was being brought from the District Hospital in Boyle to the Church of the Assumption in Collooney. Her heartbroken friends from the Healy School of Dancing carried bouquets of roses and dressed in green dancing costumes to pay tribute to their pal. Men wearing white armbands carried the small casket from the church following the funeral to the nearby cemetery where she was buried.

Bernadette's sisters, Ann and Kerri, said years later how their father believed he knew the identity of the killer. In 2002 they said that Gerry, who died in December 1999, went to his grave believing he knew who had murdered his daughter but sadly not getting any justice for her before he passed away. Ann said: "Nobody was ever arrested for it or brought to justice but we have our suspicions now. Dad knew who it was, I think, before he died. But nothing could ever be said or no one came forward. Dad was a great talker but, at the same time, something like that was very upsetting. He said he knew who it was. And I probably know too."

In a rather disturbing turn of events, all material evidence, including the young girl's bike and her mother's purse which were found at the time, were lost while in Garda custody. Evidence which, with huge strides and advancements in DNA technology, could have helped to finally solve the case.

Little Bernadette never screamed for help and was also sensible enough not to speak to strangers, which has left many people asking the question, did she know the person who offered her a lift and subsequently murdered her? Did she trust them and therefore not question their sinister motives? Or was it a stranger, a criminal or paedophile, who just happened to be passing through the remote area and saw the little girl and snatched her when nobody was around?

Journalist Brighid McLaughlin, who spent four years investigating and writing about the murder, said it was a case she worked tirelessly on in the hope of getting some answers about what could have possibly happened to Bernadette. Brighid said she first became interested in covering the tragic story while in the area with her late husband, Michael, who was from Sligo.

Recalling her initial intrigue, Brighid told me: "We used to go there a lot. Someone mentioned it to me about the Bernadette Connolly disappearance and they said it was in Collooney, so I decided I would go about contacting the family. I got talking to her father, Gerry, who was a complete gentleman, one of the nicest men you could ever meet. We met in a local pub on our own first and then he invited his daughters along too. They were all very traumatised by what had happened, even after all of those years. And Gerry was just bereft by the whole thing. He had a photographic memory of the events looking back. And I was very impressed by the way he could remember times and dates."

The well-known journalist, who sadly lost her own beloved sister Siobhan to murder in February 2006, recalled hearing of Fr Columba's offer to help the grief-stricken family. "When Bernadette went missing he actually stayed with them. Father

Columba actually moved into the tiny house with them. Himself and Gerry were inseparable. He knew everything that was going on and helped open all the letters that came to the house. People trusted the church, it was people's life back then."

Brighid spent a lot of time interviewing those in the tight-knit community about the day the little girl went missing and said there were many different accounts given to her. She said there were conflicting stories given about who was at the local monastery on the night of Bernadette's disappearance. "It was at the time of the aborted Apollo 13 landing and there were only 13 TVs in the whole town at the time. TVs weren't a big thing then. There was one in the monastery, so the congregation were all there. But missing from the room at the crucial time was Brother X and Father Columba, they had apparently gone to get petrol.

"They had taken a long winded route, a way they would normally not go. They drove a green Ford Escort, everyone would have known it locally as the monastery van. The gardaí discovered that it couldn't be accounted for at the crucial time between 4.30pm and 7.55pm on the day of Bernadette's disappearance.

"What I thought was fascinating was that Mr McTiernan, the petrol station owner, told the gardaí that Brother X had called in for petrol and had beeped on the horn. But Brother X denied he ever bought petrol there. That was the first time the gardaí looked at the monastery as far as I'm aware. Some people said he wasn't in the monastery and some said he was. They asked every monk where they were and there was a huge discrepancy in their answers. Then a black car was also seen in the vicinity on the day Bernadette went missing and the gardaí asked anyone who had seen it to come forward."

And speaking about when the remains of little Bernadette were found, Brighid said the accounts she heard from various people who lived locally were absolutely heartbreaking. She said the murder really devastated those living in the rural area. "The saddest thing is that her three miraculous medals were still pinned on her. It was just so poignant and sad, the innocence of it all. They searched the monastery as well as the rest of the area very well. There were also two men, known criminals, who were in the area at the time Bernadette went missing. Their car was seen coming from the Cloonamahon Monastery the day before she disappeared. It was chilling."

But the respected journalist said despite her best efforts she never managed to pin down who she believed was responsible for brutally murdering the innocent little girl. "I spent four years working on that story, going up and back to Sligo and I kept in touch with Gerry and the family. It was harrowing, the whole thing. Nobody knows who killed Bernadette Connolly. I found the whole thing very frustrating because nothing made sense. None of the stories fitted. All you could do was investigate it again and again and keep an open mind. There is definitely someone who knows what happened to Bernadette that day, there is no doubt about it. You can only hope that they will find it in their conscience to come forward."

Just weeks before her untimely death, the little girl wrote an essay for school called 'Myself' detailing the simple things in life which made her happy as well as her dreams and hopes for the future. In it she wrote: "My name is Bernadette Connolly. I have two sisters. I have one brother. Mary Flynn is my best friend. I want to be a teacher when I grow up. I have curly hair. I have brown eyes. I have glasses. I sit beside Patsy Kerins."

Bernadette's sister, Ann, said in 2020 that detectives investigating her case brought the family into the station to show them what evidence they had managed to gather during the course of their investigation. She said in an interview with a local newspaper: "The guards took us in eight years ago, into the station in Ballymote, and showed us all the evidence they had and that wasn't something they would usually do. The murder happened at a time with no technology or mobile phones, but they were extremely thorough. There was literally only minutes from where she was last spotted to when she was gone. It was an opportunist thing.

"It all led to one man – I know there was a lot of talk about Cloonamahon and all of that – but when they showed us the evidence it all pointed to one man, a fisherman who has died since, a known paedophile."

Ann said examining the evidence and coming to the conclusion of who she believed had taken their sister's life gave the family some closure. "The case is still open, but to us, we think it was him. That was closure to us. We went to Bernie's grave after that and we just said to her that it was the best we could do."

The tragic cases of Bernadette Connolly and Mary Boyle were in fact once connected when, in July 1994, members of An Garda Siochana travelled to Newcastle in England to discuss the possibility of child killer Robert Black's potential link to both investigations.

Detective Sergeant Aidan Murray and Inspector Michael Duffy made the trip but, on further inspection, Black was ruled out. However, years later, information would be received which placed him in the Donegal area where Mary Boyle went missing at the time.

It is believed that by the time the claims were made, Black, who had murdered four schoolgirls between 1981 and 1986, had died in prison. He was found dead in his cell in Maghaberry high-security prison in Antrim in 2016 after having a heart attack, aged 68. Sadly, the only thing that now connects the two little girls is that both cases remain open and unsolved.

# 10.

# My Father, The Paedophile

*'At the end, when he was dying, he did turn around and say he was sorry. He never said exactly what for ... I wanted to hear it for myself but he never admitted it'*

Nikita was a young child when her father Eamon Cooke was finally locked up for sexually abusing kids.

He had managed to get away with his sickening crimes for years and allegedly continued to abuse vulnerable children, despite many previous accusations being made against him.

Nikita said she didn't really get to know her father as a child because she was placed in foster care at a very young age.

She only met her father a handful of times, in a controlled environment, during planned visits. It would only be after her 18th birthday that she would finally get the chance to sit down and ask him, face to face, the questions which had always played on her mind.

That first visit would not be over coffee or during a walk in the park but rather in the confines of a prison visiting room. Her decision to see him wasn't born out of loyalty to a caring parent or to offer him some company while locked up in a Dublin prison but rather out of curiosity, to see if the man sitting in front of her was really the monster he had been portrayed to be.

Before meeting her father, Nikita had to think carefully about the decision to see him. She didn't want it to impact on the new life she had made for herself. Plus, she was aware from what people had told her of just how manipulative and evil her father was. Nikita said she had heard horrible stories about her father growing up, of his sickening crimes, and was warned on many occasions to keep her distance from the sexual predator for her own safety.

It was only after typing his name into an internet search engine that she truly learnt of the extent of Cooke's sickening crimes. "I only found out from Google what he had done. Nobody had actually ever sat me down and properly told me, 'This is your father and this is what he has done'. I never met anybody who knew him either. I knew nothing about him. I was told he was dangerous, though, so I assumed it might have been something sexual.

"But people were not willing to tell me, everyone assumed I already knew. Everybody knows their mother and father and, if you don't, you are going to search it out in order to try and find out where you came from."

Despite feeling nervous about her decision, the young woman, now 24, said there was a massive urge within her to visit 'Cooke' in jail. Strangely enough, throughout our many conversations, Nikita only referred to her father by his surname and not Eamon. When asked why, she explained the reason for it was probably due to the fact that she had no feelings for the man.

During these unsupervised visits, she said that she truly got to know what Cooke was like for the first time. And far from painting him as a saint, Nikita said her father was very much the 'monster' they said he was – a man who had a tendency for violence. But despite that, she said there are still many questions surrounding his alleged involvement in Philip's disappearance which in her mind remain unanswered.

Arbour Hill Prison, where he was based, was full of extremely dangerous criminals like her father including murderers, serial child abusers and rapists.

It was a week after turning 18 that Nikita first visited. "I remember going into the jail and asking the prison staff, 'How do I know which one he is?' I had Googled an image of him but I wasn't 100 per cent sure. As soon as he walked out, this little old man with a stick, I knew it was him. I just sat down and said to him: 'I'm your daughter,' and he appeared happy. The whole situation was very weird. He told me what he had heard about me through updates he had received."

With just a table dividing them, Nikita recalled the first conversation the pair had as prison staff watched on. "I asked him what life in prison was like and he told me how he was working in the jail library. He worked there, was allowed to smoke and he had his own TV and pictures on the wall in his cell. I was so confused. He seemed so frail and happy but I knew he was a monster and was evil. It was hard to connect the two."

Even though Cooke was serving a sentence for child abuse at the time, he never acknowledged his crimes or that he was a paedophile to her. And any time Nikita brought up the topic he would quickly change the conversation. "He would never admit to abusing children. I asked him and he just kept skimming over it.

"I visited him probably three times in prison before he was moved to the hospice. Just a few months after my last visit to him in the prison he got sick. I went to the hospice and stayed there on and off until he died."

Nikita said she had no recollection of Cooke ever touching her inappropriately when she was a child. And she said there was no medical evidence to suggest that he had interfered with her after she was examined and questioned by social services before being placed in care at a very young age. She said she was perhaps one of the very few lucky children who escaped his evil clutches.

As to whether her father was involved in one of Ireland's most high-profile unsolved missing persons cases, Nikita said she fully acknowledged that Cooke was a twisted child molester but said she struggled to believe he abducted Philip despite, in her words, being capable of it.

From the short time she got to know him, she said that in her mind there were too many unanswered questions and very little hard evidence to connect him to the case.

Reflecting on her relationship with her father growing up, Nikita recalled how he would break the rules and visit her unaccompanied when he wasn't supposed to. "I wouldn't have known him very well. I would have only known what it said in the papers about him when I was older and from what I had heard about him, that he was a paedophile who manipulated people and how he was just not a nice man.

"I have one memory from when I was young when he did come and visit me at my foster home. He wasn't allowed to, but he did. I had obviously been told growing up 'don't go near him, he's dangerous' so I had this impression in my head of what he was like and so I didn't have very much interaction with him."

Rekindling the relationship, she said, wasn't likely to change the way she viewed her father. "To be honest I didn't really identify with him as being my father. He's the person who made me but I don't really see him as a father figure or anything like that, I only see him for what he did and what he was. I have no real emotion towards him. I know the facts and I know what he did."

Cooke was always trying to portray himself as a saint, someone who looked out for the vulnerable in the community. It was a mask Nikita believes he wore in public to deflect from the horrific acts he was committing on young children. "I think he tried to make himself look like a hero in a lot of aspects of his life but that was just to fool people.

"He would have interacted with guards and hacked the system to see where they were and he would have turned up at the scene straight away. He wanted to know everything and be seen as the hero."

Her father often preyed on vulnerable children who were easy to get close to and abuse and Nikita said in order to not draw suspicion of such sickening acts he would also carry out public displays of charity in the local community so that nobody would ever question his inappropriate close contact with kids. "He would have bought a lot of toys and stuff for charities and he would have gone to the local hospital and dropped off toys, he would have done things like that to be part of the community but that was obviously just a way to get close to the kids.

"A lot of the kids in our area would try and play in our house, which was like a dumping ground, so the kids would mess around in there and he would be willing to let them in so he could get closer to them. So I knew he was the kind of person that would put himself in those situations to get close to kids."

When he was diagnosed with terminal cancer, Cooke was transferred to St Francis Hospice in Dublin and Nikita spent the last few days with him before he died.

While under palliative care, the child molester, who was now skin and bone, spent the majority of his time sleeping due to the heavy medication he was on. But while awake, Nikita said he struggled to hold a conversation.

As well as having terminal lung cancer, his daughter is also adamant he had Alzheimer's Disease. She said she first noticed a change in him months earlier, during one of her jail visits. His mind was quickly deteriorating, she told me, and by the time he ended up in the hospice he would often even forget who he was. She said he would often spend hours watching the cartoon SpongeBob SquarePants in Irish.

It was during this time, in 2016, that gardaí received information from a former female victim of Cooke's that she had witnessed him hit Philip over the head at his Dublin radio station and officers decided to quiz him over the claims. Detectives arrived at the hospice and interviewed Cooke, on two separate occasions, as best they could and were allowed to in his debilitated state. But he was highly medicated and slipping in and out of consciousness. Due to the lung cancer, he had also developed a nasty, persistent cough and often gasped for air. It's believed the 79-year-old only managed to give 'yes' and 'no' answers to many of the questions put to him by the two detectives.

He reportedly confirmed to the officers who visited him that he had met Philip but gave no further indication as to whether he was involved in the schoolboy's abduction. Nikita, who was asked to leave Cooke's bedside while the interviews took place, believes her father would have probably agreed to anything the officers asked him due to his physical and mental state at the time. But she said had detectives got to him sooner he may have answered more of their questions in greater detail.

"He had Alzheimer's before he even entered the hospice. He didn't even know who he was by then. When I visited him in prison, I remember asking him for a pen and he handed me a lighter and told me to write with it. So when I went to the hospice I had to remind him again who I was.

"Most of the time he would just sleep from all the medication he was on. We would watch SpongeBob in Irish and he would tell me he loved the show but he didn't know any Irish. He would tell me he was going to be on the TV soon, he was obviously hallucinating. They definitely waited too long to ask him. If they had approached him earlier then they might have got a decent enough answer out of him. Would he have been honest, though, if asked? The answer is probably no. He wouldn't admit to being a paedophile, so even if he was involved with Philip's disappearance he was probably never going to admit it."

Elaborating on her father's state of mind during the questioning, she added: "He would whisper and grab the air in front of him, which I found quite disturbing. He would just talk about random stuff. None of it made sense to be honest and when the guards came in to interview him I said to them: 'He doesn't even know who he is, let alone anything else'. He was just going to go along with what he was asked because he didn't know any different. I could have told him we were going to Spain the next day and he would have agreed with me. He would have agreed with anything."

Even if her father had any role to play in the teenager's abduction and suspected murder, Nikita believes he would always have taken any dark secrets to his grave. His daughter said he was manipulative and self-absorbed and would most likely have teased gardaí when confronted about his possible involvement in Philip's case rather than open up about it.

Cooke owned multiple properties in Dublin over the years including one in Aylesbury, Tallaght, a short distance away from where Philip was abducted on Ballyroan Road in Rathfarnham. He also owned a house in Clondalkin as well as numerous houses in Inchicore, where his pirate station studio for Radio Dublin was located, over the years. He also had plots of land around the country including in Kilmacteige, Co Sligo and in the foothills of the Dublin Mountains. Some areas of land were searched by officers but turned up nothing, according to a source. For many investigating the case, as well those who knew Cooke, this particular stretch of ground has always raised suspicion due to the fact the paedophile had managed to bury a large 20-foot container under the ground. The strange reasoning behind its concealment has never been discovered but it's believed to have been used to hide and store incriminating evidence against him over the years.

Nikita ultimately believes that – apart from the woman who came forward claiming to have witnessed Cooke hit Philip at Radio Dublin – there is nothing tangible to tie him to the crime and until she is told otherwise, she will find it hard to believe he was directly involved.

But in order to rule him out as a possible suspect, and his name no longer to be linked to the case, Nikita suggests that gardaí should search all land and property he ever owned. By doing so she believes it would categorically prove once and for all if he was behind the teenager's abduction or not – even though he would have hidden any incriminating evidence very well. Nikita believes he would have dug up a piece of land in order to bury it and would have been easily able to do so as he had access to a JCB and owned so many plots of land and property at the time.

Nikita said there was one property Cooke had access to, a few years after Philip's disappearance, which she believes may hold vital evidence if he was involved. She said it could be under the foundations of the property as he was carrying out renovations on it at the time.

Despite not having access to it until years after Philip's disappearance, she said he could have easily moved any damning evidence and placed it under the ground at the house he was working on before building on top of it. "If he had any information to do with Philip or anything else, he would have made sure it was buried. Under the foundations of a house or in a container. If I were to search anywhere I would have searched this one property he owned a few years after Philip went missing. If there's anything got to do with anything he wouldn't have kept it so out in the open. He would have put it under the foundations of that house. I found it weird that they (the guards) were searching fields and not that property."

Nikita pointed out that Cooke had plenty of places to hide evidence against him if necessary, either in 1986 or in the years that followed. And she said there would have been nothing stopping him moving it from place to place. "He had land in Sligo as well. I would fully dig that up and check too. There is no point looking in small places, you are going to have to rip the house up to see if there is any evidence that he knew anything about it. There were a lot of properties he owned over the years which he later sold too. He owned a good few houses."

Cooke was a sadistic child abuser who left a trail of devastation behind him when he died on June 4, 2016. He was accused of molesting numerous children over the years and often described by many who knew him as someone who could lose his temper at the drop of a hat.

While not believing her father had a role to play in Philip's disappearance, Nikita said it was highly probable that he may have known who did, especially if it was another child abuser. She said even if he knew their identity, however, he would never have admitted it to the authorities.

"Everyone knows how evil he was. Even after he was prosecuted for being a paedophile he never would have acknowledged that. I am sure there are hundreds of people out there who have come across him and never spoken up about it," she said.

"At the end, when he was dying, he did turn around and say he was sorry. He never said exactly what for but it was obviously for being a paedophile. I tried to bring it up loads of times with him, about being a paedophile, but he never replied. I would have said 'did you do this?' when asking him about certain cases. I obviously knew that he was prosecuted for it but I wanted to hear it for myself but he never admitted it to me."

Nikita said she was shocked when her father's name was first publicly linked to Philip's disappearance in 2016. "Initially I thought they were trying to pin this on a dying man but then I asked: 'Could it have happened? Did it happen?' But then I thought no."

Cooke was smart when it came to covering his tracks and he always tried to think 10 steps ahead. Nikita said although he was very capable of molesting a child, he was more interested in gratifying his sick sexual urges than committing murder. "I don't think he would have just killed someone. I think people got on the wrong side of him and he obviously did stuff back to them but I don't think he would have put himself in a situation like that. It would have been too dangerous and he looked out to protect himself, so I don't think he would have been stupid enough."

Despite it being suggested that he might have possibly hit out at the teenager for rejecting his advances, Nikita believes

Cooke was so selfish that he wouldn't have bothered retaliating. "If he did do it, it would have been by mistake. I don't think he would have intentionally planned it out. He was a paedophile, he wanted to be around kids and he wasn't going to do anything to jeopardise that.

"It's possible that he ran a competition and did meet Philip at some point at the radio station. I'm sure if he was rejected (by Philip) he would have just moved on to the next child. He abused so many kids that he would have just moved to the next child, not killed them. I don't think it was to do with the sex of the child either. He abused so many kids that I don't believe that came into it. I think he was more a case of, 'I will abuse a child if I can'. I think his main concern was getting caught. Most of the kids he would have abused would have been from around the area he lived."

Nikita's belief also is that Cooke would have been too smart to drop the schoolboy's bag back himself in the laneway if he was behind young Philip's abduction. "He had enough kids to do that. He had access to them. He would have bribed them with sweets and said: 'Here, drop that up'. He knew how to manipulate and threaten them too. It might have even been a case of just giving a teenager a few smokes to do it."

Nikita recalled how she was at the hospice on the night Cooke died and said it was a horrible experience – one which she will never forget. "I was there when he took his last breath. It was terrifying. I had been outside and went back into the room and the nurse said to me, 'It's happening'. He turned around and said: 'I'm sorry'. He was gasping for air and groaning. I emptied his pockets after he had passed away and there was a photo of me in his shirt pocket. It was destroyed as a pen had burst all over it. He always had a small notebook and pen on him too. It had a list of people who he wanted to put on his prison visitation list."

Following his death, Cooke was buried in an unmarked grave at Glasnevin Cemetery. A number of family members, including Nikita, attended the service. "There were only a handful of people there. I had literally just finished my Leaving Cert exam and was at his funeral a few hours later. At the time it was all over the radio and TV so it was hard to get away from."

For the paedophile's daughter there are still so many questions about her father which remain unanswered.

"I wish he had told me if he did do it (take Philip) so that the Cairns family could know and they would no longer have to wonder. I would have gone straight to the guards with any information I had. They deserve answers after all these years, it's heartbreaking."

# 11.

# Under The
# Microscope

*'There Eamon was in a JCB and he had
a huge mound of earth dug to the right
of a huge hole. He was in a JCB up in
the mountains by himself in the dark.
I just thought it was incredibly creepy'*

Following Cooke's death in June, 2016, many people, including
a number of detectives who worked on the investigation, were
left feeling perplexed and extremely frustrated as they were
left with even more questions than answers. Did the convicted
paedophile have a role to play in Philip's abduction? If so, did
he kill him and where did he bury the young boy's remains?

Despite best efforts by detectives, the child abuser refused to reveal any involvement in the teenager's abduction. He is alleged to have admitted knowing the schoolboy and also corroborated certain aspects of the female witness's statement. However, he point blank would not say if he kidnapped young Philip or murdered him. Nor would he reveal, if he did kill the teenager, where his remains were buried. The master manipulator, despite being just days away from death, is believed to have given them just enough information to raise serious suspicion among investigating officers, but not enough to definitively rule him as the person responsible.

Due to Cooke's deteriorating health, detectives were only able to interview him twice by his bedside about Philip's disappearance. Despite him being one of the worst child abusers the country had ever seen, he was still entitled to a duty of care and a nurse closely observed his condition while officers quizzed him about the claims which had been made against him. The whole situation proved very frustrating, especially when officers were potentially so close to determining once and for all if he had a role to play in the teenager's disappearance. Even though he did not admit to having any role in the boy's disappearance, the child abuser revealed enough that he is still deemed a suspect in the case. In fact, to some he is still the number one suspect.

I have interviewed those who knew Cooke, including former colleagues, his daughter, one of his victims and detectives who worked on the case, to try to determine if in fact he was capable of such a heinous crime. Each and every one of them had a difference of opinion as to whether they believe he was involved in Philip's abduction or not and to what extent. While some detectives who worked on the case over the years believe

Cooke was more than likely the person who snatched Philip, others – including the child abuser's own daughter, Nikita – believe it is unlikely he had a role to play.

Regardless of people's conflicting opinions, there is certainly a lot of circumstantial evidence which can't be overlooked which ties Cooke to possibly being involved in Philip's case. To begin with, there has always been speculation over whether Cooke would have even been remotely interested in kidnapping Philip as it has been long assumed that the prolific paedophile was only interested in young girls. However, I have discovered that this is not the case and there were allegedly a number of young boys who he targeted over the years, who never reported it to the authorities.

There was one young boy in particular who reportedly made a statement about the monster to authorities alleging he had abused him, only to later withdraw it. Siobhan Kennedy-McGuinness confirmed that it's actually the biggest misconception about him. She said: "It didn't matter if you were male or female. He abused hundreds of kids, it was like passing the parcel."

At the time of Philip's disappearance, Cooke would have been living in the suburb of Inchicore, a small area originally known for its railway works and located approximately five kilometres west of the city centre.

He only purchased a house in Tallaght, which is a stone's throw away from where Philip went missing in Rathfarnham, in 1987, according to documents I have seen. He later bought another property in Clondalkin in 1990.

However, during the course of my investigation into Cooke, I have been told by numerous sources that the paedophile often rented properties and is believed to have had access to one in Tallaght in 1986, the same year Philip vanished, placing him closer to the suspected abduction site. And according to one source he is also believed to have had more properties including one in Wexford, Rathfarnham and Crumlin over the years. He often bought and rented properties under various names too in order to avoid the taxman, including Richard and Joseph Cooke. According to his daughter, it was something he did quite often. Another source who knew the abuser also revealed that he allegedly had several offshore bank accounts with Danske Bank and Halifax UK to name but two, in order to hide his money.

Many people have questioned what would have brought Cooke close to the Rathfarnham area on the day Philip disappeared.

Firstly, there is the witness's statement that he had promised to give Philip a tour of the radio station and was therefore picking him up. And when it comes to the one possible sighting of Philip on the day he was reported missing, a local man gave a description of a man which strikes a remarkable likeness to Cooke.

The eyewitness told officers in 1986 how he saw a teenager fitting Philip's description talking to a man in a red car who was described as being in his 50s with grey sticky-up hair. This would have fitted the paedophile's appearance at the time. The witness also claimed the driver of the vehicle in which the teenager was leaning into was a red or wine-coloured vehicle. At the time the paedophile was known for buying, fixing up and selling cars. I have learned that he also had access to a red car in 1986, with one source claiming he owned one, and have obtained pictures which show the child abuser standing beside a vehicle fitting this description. Some of the license plate letters and numbers also match those given by the eyewitness on the day of the disappearance. Was it Cooke in the car that day on the Ballyroan Road or someone completely different who just happened to fit a similar description?

When it comes to whether Cooke was even capable of murdering someone, there is also divided opinion. Many of those who knew the monster, including Siobhan, believe he was more than capable of kidnapping and killing Philip. And she revealed how years before his alleged involvement in the teen's kidnapping, she got to experience first-hand how the paedophile would lure his unsuspecting victims back to the Radio Dublin studio. She explained how children, including herself, were used as bait to coax other kids into his flashy car. She said Cooke would often have children in his luxury Jaguar and believes it is quite possible that's how he managed to convince young Philip to come with him on the day he disappeared, if he was in fact involved. If a child or a couple of kids were already in Cooke's car, a smart teenager who might normally not get into a vehicle with a stranger on their own might deem it safe if other youngsters are already there, according to Siobhan.

Siobhan told me how Cooke once used her as a pawn to try to get a young school friend back to the decrepit run-down station. She said she remembered the day as if it was yesterday and how the hot leather seats in his Jaguar, which had Radio Dublin emblazoned across its side, would burn the backs of her little legs.

"I remember there was one particular time he asked me

what school I went to and if I ever got to see my school friends. He said: 'I can drop you down if you want to meet one of your friends and bring her up to the radio station'. That's what he would do, he would use one child to lure other children. Cooke could have easily convinced him (Philip) and said: 'Sure, you will only be a few minutes'. My parents thought I was playing out the back when in fact I was down on James Street in Cooke's car. If you had knocked at my parents' door at the time and asked where I was they would have said: 'She's playing out the back,' but I wasn't."

Siobhan said he also used to make her hide in his car in case anyone she knew spotted the pair together. "He would tell me to lie down in the back seat of the car and would cover me with a tartan wool blanket until we passed our neighbours and my family home." If he was involved in Philip's disappearance, did he make the teen also do this so nobody would spot him?

And she believes if he abducted Philip he would have most likely tried to use a child who was known to Philip as that was his MO. She said this is the only aspect of the case which would make her doubt his involvement. But according to the woman's statement she was in the car with Cooke at the time. Perhaps that was enough to make Philip feel secure about getting into the vehicle?

Did Cooke spot the teenager and offer to give him a tour of the studio on the pretence that he would then drop him to school afterwards? Did he mention another teenager's name who he may have known to put him at ease?

Philip was a well-behaved boy who would not have missed school either and if he did have plans to skip his afternoon classes and go and tour the station, surely he would have told someone of his plans? Or did Cooke promise that he would have him back at the school before anyone would even really notice he was gone?

Siobhan has no doubt Cooke was part of a larger paedophile ring that was operating in Dublin and she said if he didn't have any direct involvement in Philip's disappearance he may have known who did. "I believe he procured children for other people too. I believe he was involved in a bigger network. There is no doubt in my mind that there was a paedophile ring and they all knew what they were doing but kept schtum. So many people were afraid of him. He always went to disadvantaged areas. He used to go down and give out toys and Easter eggs. Until my dying day I will still think he had some hand in that (Philip's disappearance). Without a doubt. He fooled a lot of people. He didn't mix with people, he didn't have friends. The amount of people who he affected in Inchicore alone, and that was just my small little area."

However, there are those who believe Cooke, despite being a prolific paedophile, was unlikely to have kidnapped and killed Philip. His own daughter being one of them. Nikita said he would abuse any child he could get his hands on but would not have wanted to attract any untoward attention by taking the young boy's life.

Cooke, by his own admission, was intrigued by Philip Cairns and his case. In documents I have unearthed dating back to 2001, the pervert sensationally wrote how he had helped to search for the teenager and how he went above and beyond to try to help find him.

The convicted child abuser even said he reported suspicious tyre tracks he noticed close to land he rented in Stepaside, South

Dublin, two days after the 13-year-old's disappearance. In the startling admissions, he wrote: "Back in the '80s, I rented a piece of land at Stepaside for one of the radio transmitters and a large number of the staff gave help when concrete arrived on site.

"I was to spend months up and down to Stepaside to try and improve the signal there and most times I would go in an old jeep through Ticknock Forest. Two days after the disappearance of a young schoolboy, Philip Kearns [sic], in the area, I went up to Stepaside and saw the tracks of an ordinary car through the forest. I could not drive my own car there at that time as there was no push whatever. There were no forestry workers in the area so my first thought was the missing boy.

"On my way home, I called into Rathfarnham station to tell them of the car tracks. They said they had a lot of reports of the boy being seen and they would follow my report up as well. No one ever did and I spent the next year searching most of the mountainside but found nothing. I still believe that there is some connection between the car tracks and the missing boy who was never found."

Cooke also mentioned a young woman who he claimed helped him in his searches. I have tracked down the woman he names in the document but despite my best efforts have not been able to get in contact with her.

My main aim was to see if she could corroborate the details mentioned by Cooke. Was he telling the truth or had the paedophile made the whole thing up? She may also be able to account for his movements on the day Philip disappeared as she appears to have spent a lot of time in his company at the time. The woman in question may possibly possess information which could either rule Cooke out as a potential suspect or put him smack bang in the middle of being involved in the teenager's abduction. There are a number of individuals mentioned in the document, who were juveniles at the time, who I believe may prove beneficial for the gardaí to track down and talk to about Cooke and his interest in the boy. I have forwarded them onto the authorities with the hope that they will follow up on them.

In the documents in which Cooke made the unusual admissions, he was writing about his life, his upbringing and his time at Radio Dublin. His remarks about the missing schoolboy stick out like a sore thumb as they bear no relevance to the story he is telling. So why include them, and in such great detail?

You also have to put the claims into context. They were made in 2001, a whole 15 years before his name would ever be attached to Philip's case. Was Cooke teasing the authorities? Did he abduct the boy on that cold day back in 1986? If he didn't take Philip, did he know who had? Or was he merely trying to give the impression that he was an individual who cared for children?

A detective who knew Cooke told me that he was the type of individual who "liked to leave bread crumbs" in order to antagonise authorities. And he said he would often tease officers by alluding to his crimes but never fully admitting to them. Is this what he was doing here in this document which was for a civil matter?

A former detective, who worked on the case, examined the documents and said he found the reference particularly obscure. He told me: "The mention of Philip Cairns is very unusual. Cooke is either referencing the teenager to further paint himself as a concerned individual who cared for children or there is something more sinister to these references. It's very hard to tell either way but they merit further investigation."

Philip's mother said in an interview in 2016, when Cooke's name was first linked to the case, that if the paedophile was involved in his disappearance that he would have perhaps coerced him into his car as he didn't know the DJ. "He wasn't big into music. His main hobby was going fishing with Phil (his father). He took an interest in it but he wouldn't be dying to go and see a radio station and wouldn't have taken time off school to go. He wouldn't have mitched, no way. He was put into a car or unless he (Cooke) talked him into the car. He could have said: 'I'm a DJ. I'll give you a lift. I'm going up there,' and used his celebrity status to coax him in or maybe Philip could tell his friends: 'Look who I got a lift with,' but I don't even know if (Cooke) was well known at the time. He definitely wouldn't have taken off school. He was a good child. He was coaxed or forced."

Cooke knew the Dublin Mountains like the back of his hand and for many who knew him, if he was involved in Philip's disappearance he would have most likely hidden any incriminating evidence in a pocket of land he either owned or knew very little people had access to.

Radio boss Kevin Branigan said he once saw Cooke in a JCB on a cold dark night with a mound of earth beside him close to Ticknock on the foothills of the Dublin Mountains. He said he reported the unusual sighting to gardaí in 2016 following the revelations connecting him to the case. Speaking about his first encounter with Cooke at Radio Dublin, he told me: "I was involved in pirate radio in the mid-Eighties and early Nineties. I was doing a radio show at Radio Dublin, I was only 16. I was only with the station for about three months. There was a small pirate radio scene in the early Nineties that would have been on the air, in people's garden sheds and stuff, more as a hobby. Eamon Cooke was still on air with Radio Dublin at the time. Around 1991 to 1993, Eamon used to broadcast this programme on a Sunday afternoon where he would go on for an hour and would basically spread scandal and innuendo about others who were involved in the radio industry. There would have been a lot of paranoia going on in his mind, thinking that all these small pirate stations were out to get him. It was like he was always looking for a fight.

"We had a station called NSR105 coming from Stillorgan and Eamon was interfering with our signal from a transmission site he had set up in Saggart. We tracked it down one Saturday evening. I was only about 21 at the time and had no other intent other than to see if he had antennas there. It was starting to get dark as it was around six or seven o'clock. You would drive up this laneway and on the left was where his site was. There Eamon was in a JCB and he had a huge mound of earth dug to the right of a huge hole. He was in a JCB up the mountains by himself in the dark. I just thought it was incredibly creepy.

"We sat for a bit watching him and he spotted us and started to drive towards us in the JCB, so we drove off. He went on the show the next day to say he had seen us. Why would he be up there in the dark and cold in a JCB by himself? I was wondering what he had dug the hole for and decided to drive up a week later and all the muck was gone and the piece of ground was covered over."

The CEO of Radio Nova and Classic Hits said since it emerged that Cooke was a possible suspect in the Cairns case, the image he witnessed that night had played over and over in his mind. "I have thought about it a few times over the years. When I read articles about Philip Cairns being possibly connected to Cooke I decided to ring the police. I rang a good few times and eventually after a few weeks a detective rang me and he asked me to show him the site.

"I brought him up to the area and we went over to the land, which is now just a field full of rough grass and rocks. You could see that the grass in the place where I had seen him dig the hole that night was all growing in a different direction to the grass that was growing around it. I described to the detective what I saw and that was the last I ever heard about it." He does not believe the land was searched following the visit to the site. "What the detective said at the time was in order for them to perform a dig, they needed evidence. He said it seemed a bit suspicious. I have driven up a few times since to see if it has been dug up but as far as I could see it hadn't."

Even as a young boy, Kevin was obsessed with radio and at the age of 12 he begged his mother to bring him to the house where the Radio Dublin studio was located in Inchicore. And he recalled the chaotic scene which awaited them when they arrived.

"The door opened and there were kids everywhere. We asked if there was any chance we could look around. And then at the end of the hallway, out came Eamon. This man in a string vest. He came out and looked and then walked back into the room he had been in. I didn't think anything of it but years later my mother said she found it strange that it was only when he saw her that he went back into the room and closed the door slowly behind him. She thought that was exceptionally creepy. A few years later, when I was 16 and doing a show on a Saturday, from seven to nine, my dad used to drive me and would wait outside until I was done. I thought it was because he didn't want me having to make the long journey on the bus to the station but he told me years later that he only did it as he believed the place wasn't safe."

A number of people who knew Cooke at the time have backed up suggestions that the child abuser knew the Dublin Mountains like the back of his hand and that if he hid anything it's most likely there. One told me: "Cooke knew every inch of the mountains. He was always up there fixing his radio equipment. God knows what he has hidden up there."

In 2016, while being questioned by officers on his deathbed, a DNA sample was taken from Cooke to be cross-referenced against those which had been left on Philip's grey satchel. But according to news reports at the time no DNA belonging to Cooke was found on the bag when it was re-tested. Despite this claim, Cooke cannot be ruled out of the investigation. Many detectives who have worked on the investigation over the years still believe the theory he may have got one of his young victims to plant the satchel back in the laneway, therefore not touching it. There's also the possibility that his DNA is amongst the mixed samples which can't be tested. To many who worked on the case, this is the most plausible possibility.

According to retired Garda Cold Case Detective Alan Bailey, Cooke was extremely clever and may not in fact have touched the bag. Bailey also pointed out how the handling of evidence back in the Eighties was not as stringent as it is nowadays and there is a high possibility that some DNA may have been destroyed in the process. Bailey, who worked on the case, believes Cooke would have known not to touch the schoolboy's bag for fear of leaving any evidence, including fingerprints, on it.

"The problem with that bag, and we had it in other cold cases, is that the bag wouldn't have been handled then the way it would be now. It's not through any carelessness, it's just the way it was at the time. You might get fingerprints on a book or a handle of a bag but you might not find a fingerprint on the bag itself. The fact there was no DNA to link him (Cooke) would not surprise me."

However, as has been explained, there is still the probability that it is amongst the mixed DNA samples on the bag and he cannot be ruled out of the investigation.

In 2016, a source close to Cooke revealed to me how he was always fascinated by the case and would often comment on it when it was in the papers or on TV. "Years after Philip went missing, Cooke would often say he went out and helped search for him. He said at the time that everyone did. But he always said there would 'never be a trace of that young fella'.

"Anytime the case was on the TV or news he would also comment on how it was incredible his schoolbag had just magically reappeared, making out it was some form of magic that was performed to get it back to the laneway in which it was found."

It was also claimed at the time that Cooke had left a cryptic note in one of his old lock-ups which was discovered following his death. The handwritten note, which is believed to have been written by the paedophile in jail in either 2014 or 2015, reportedly stated the author was "sorry for what I did to Philip". Along with the note, hundreds of video tapes, mini discs and documents were also found in the storage unit in West Dublin.

It was reportedly handed over to officers by a member of Cooke's family once they realised what it said. A source close to Cooke said at the time how he would have put things into the 24-hour storage facility while out on bail and also when he had his convictions overturned. He had also kept newspaper clippings from over the years. He had highlighted sections of the articles which mentioned his sick crimes. A person who worked at the lock-up said Cooke had rented the storage unit since 2006. The source also alleged Cooke had underground bunkers at properties he owned over the years and owned a property in Rathfarnham at the time Philip disappeared.

A source close to Cooke also told me in 2016 how the paedophile was a strange character who used to go off with shovels to dig up land, stating he was off to bury the pet dog, despite not owning one. The source said at the time: "The family didn't own a dog. What was he doing with the shovel? What was he digging? At the time nothing was thought about it but looking back it was strange." The source also suggested if Cooke murdered Philip he was more than likely behind others and he should be investigated for other missing children cases in areas and places he would have visited, including in Northern Ireland, where he visited two or three times a year.

Then there is the question of the vast amount of wealth he had accumulated over the years. A lot of people who knew Cooke, including his own daughter, are unsure how he amassed such large sums of money considering he only worked for a pirate radio station. In 2016, one source close to Cooke said questions needed to be asked as to how he was "close to being a millionaire." He added: "The belief is it came from a paedophile ring. He used to go to the pub every couple of weeks, despite never drinking. You have to ask why. He had land and property everywhere."

A former colleague at Radio Dublin, James Dillon, believes Cooke was more than capable of kidnapping and killing Philip. Dillon believes he was an evil individual and said despite no concrete evidence against him, he shouldn't be ruled out as a suspect. "He had a definite leaning towards violence and a threatening streak, and he had a record of picking children up and having other children in the car. He very seldom tried to pick somebody up in the car on his own from what we could see and have come to know since.

"His modus operandi of having the radio station name on the side of the car was a potential magnet too. And then having one or more children in the car, it would have looked reasonably innocent. The fact that Philip Cairns may have been picked up (by Cooke) certainly seems credible to me but I don't have any direct evidence. Would I believe him to be capable of it? Absolutely. I wouldn't doubt that at all. Whoever did it was clever enough to have covered their tracks for a long time and that was one of his hallmarks."

Dillon said the reasons why Cooke buried a 20-foot container under the ground on his land in the Dublin Mountains also raises many questions. "One of the stories that I came across accidentally, which doesn't prove anything one way or another, was that he had electricity in that container.

"I was talking to a guy who worked in the ESB and he asked me if I had ever come across this guy called Cooke and I said 'yeah'. He said there was an anomaly up near the field where he had the container buried. They assumed that Cooke had pulled some kind of power supply from the main electricity. It turned out that when they climbed the pole they found the connection but that the cable had gone down through the pole and into this container underground. He had this whole thing, the container, buried with an electric supply which wasn't official."

And it's not just Cooke's former colleagues and victims who believe he may be behind the longest unsolved missing person case in Ireland. An ex-wife, who did not wish to be named, told me how he was often violent towards her when they were married. "Eamon Cooke was one of the most evil people I have ever met in my life. Has Cooke killed anyone? I really don't know. Was he capable of doing so? Yes." She added: "I didn't know Cooke when Philip went missing but Cooke did say he knew him when the story was on the news."

The missing teenager's mother is unsure whether Cooke had a role to play in her son's disappearance. For her, too many unanswered questions remain.

Speaking on RTE Radio in 2016, Alice explained how she felt when she heard the revelations surrounding Cooke. "I didn't like it but I was hoping it wasn't true. I still don't know what the story is and if it's true or not. You can't think too much either about it because you could waste your whole life feeling bad about that person. I don't think too much about it at all." She added: "The man is dead now. May the Lord have mercy on his soul. You still have to forgive, haven't you? For me to have my own peace, I'd have to forgive."

When asked if she wished officers had got more answers

from Cooke on his deathbed, she said: "I do feel it was a bit late in the day."

But Alice said she understood why the woman with the vital information only came forward when she did. "She was probably traumatised and maybe didn't think it was going to happen, that he was going to die and maybe it's only when she heard that he was dying that she felt she had to do something about it. I don't know. I certainly think Philip was abducted anyway, after that I don't know. I have no idea. It's only recently that I've come to terms that he probably won't come back, possibly since my husband died. He was always waiting and hoping too, but I think he gave up thinking he was going to see him again, much quicker than I did."

Returning to the subject of Cooke's possible involvement in Philip's disappearance, Alice said: "We always knew where Philip was until the day he disappeared. He always came straight home from school. Unless Eamon Cooke picked up Philip on the day. I don't think he had any communication with him at all before that. Whatever happened with Philip, it happened on that day."

In a separate interview around the same time, she said Philip was starting to get into music but had never spoken of Cooke. "Philip was only sort of getting into music but he wouldn't have been that involved that he would be going to radio stations. He never mentioned him (Cooke) and, as far as I know, he didn't know him. I never saw him (Cooke) before and never heard Philip talk about him. He'd hardly ever been in the local record shop.

"I'm glad the gardaí are following any line of investigation because it shows they are determined to find out what happened.

I'm open minded about it (the Cooke involvement). I would be worried that if this new lead didn't amount to anything, then people might still think that the case is kind of closed and they might not come forward with information and then a person who might be responsible for it might be more than likely to get away."

She went on: "The gardaí came to me a number of weeks ago and told us they were examining a new line of enquiry, but did not mention Eamon Cooke by name. They said they were going to interview this person. I think it was a few days later they came back and said that the first day they went to him he said he knew Philip or had been in his company, but then when they went back again a second time and he denied knowing him at all," she told the *Evening Herald*.

And in 2020, when asked about the Cooke connection for a Scannal RTE documentary, Philip's eldest sister, Mary said she was of the belief that he was not involved in her brother's disappearance. "We knew about Eamon Cooke a long time before it came out … but ultimately the timeline didn't match."

Despite the mounting evidence against Cooke, he went to his grave leaving many questions unanswered. Was he involved in Philip's abduction? Did he act alone? Or was he not behind the teenager's abduction and any evidence pointing towards him is merely coincidental.

Despite dying in June 2016, one detective told me that he believes the paedophile is still the main suspect. "Down through the years there have been several persons of interest, all of which have been interviewed or enquired into but, due to a lack of evidence, were brought no further. But if new information came in today they would re-emerge as people of interest and be looked into further. Cooke to me remains as the number one suspect in the case."

There are a few aspects surrounding the theory of Cooke being a potential suspect which have raised questions since his death.

Cooke was in court, along with four other men, on October 21, 1986, after being charged with throwing a petrol bomb at a house on the South Circular Road. He is said to have organised the petrol-bombing of the home of former employee John Paul O'Toole. It's alleged he was targeted for being with a female known to Cooke and was jealous of this fact. His sentencing was deferred until November 3. He received a four-year suspended sentence.

Would Cooke have been willing to chance abducting Philip on October 23rd, in between his two court hearings? Some people who knew Cooke have suggested that the time frame would have made it unlikely for him to carry out such a daring abduction while others, including one of his victims, believe he would have tried to abuse as many kids as possible before potentially being locked up for a long period of time.

One person who got to know Cooke after he was named as a possible suspect is retired Detective Sergeant Tom Doyle. Doyle first arrived at Rathfarnham Garda Station in 1998 and took over the teenager's case file almost immediately. He decided not to rely solely on other officers' recollections of the investigation and took it upon himself to go back and re-examine every shred of evidence – witness statements, as well as anything pertaining to the case. He wanted to look at everything with a fresh set of eyes. It wasn't that he didn't trust his predecessor's stringent work, but he wanted to get a true sense of the massive task at hand. Doyle talked to colleagues who would have worked on the early investigation, quizzing them on every aspect of the case. He re-interviewed witnesses, read through hundreds of statements which were taken from locals at the time and over the years and, of course, met with Philip's heartbroken family.

Doyle said that from the moment he met Philip's loved ones he instantly became determined to try to solve the case. He said that despite having to contend with numerous other murders, robberies and other serious crimes in the area, Philip's case never drifted far from his mind. And he said that Philip's mother held no hatred in her heart towards her son's abductor, she just wanted her little boy home. "I have to say that when I met the family I became passionate about wanting to do the best that I could do to solve this mystery. They are just the loveliest, most wonderful family. They absolutely deserve resolution to this, for that one person to come forward.

"They hold no grievance against those involved. In fact, Alice once told me if she knew where her son was, she wouldn't hold anything against the person involved. She said she would actually forgive that person and move on because the family would have closure in knowing where Philip is. That is what they are looking for, they are not looking for retribution or revenge, they are not looking for people to be locked up for the rest of their lives in prison, they just want their little boy home, that is all they are looking for.

"When I got involved in this case I said to myself, 'Right, for as long as I'm going to be here I'm going to give this my best shot'. I would have loved to have brought the family some solace and closure before I retired but unfortunately, despite thousands of statements that were taken, thousands of interviews conducted and places we excavated, it didn't happen.

"We had people over the years come forward wanting to take responsibility, claiming involvement, only for it to later transpire they had psychological issues, for example, and it wasn't them. We interviewed so many people in the hope that they could add something to the investigation but it never came. Well, not until the information came in about Cooke."

Doyle interviewed Cooke twice on his deathbed in the hope of getting some form of admission from the paedophile and said that the investigation team had planned to interview him a third time – only to be informed that the child abuser had died.

Speaking for the first time about the time he came face to face with the paedophile at St Francis Hospice, the former detective said it was a chilling experience which he would never forget.

Recalling his encounter with Cooke, he told me: "When interviewing him on his deathbed, some of his comments sent chills down my spine. I would link what he said with the person who came forward in 2016. She was absolutely credible and I think what he told me on his deathbed lends to her credibility in a very big way. And on the basis of that, I would certainly think he should remain a suspect and I would like to think that everything possible surrounding Eamon Cooke has been looked at or, if it hasn't, should still be considered a subject to be looked at."

He continued: "We interviewed him and planned to take it further and then we learnt that he had passed away. We had set aside plans for other people to go in and conduct the interviews, someone other than me. Some people will respond to a certain way of interviewing and others to another so we were going to try it with someone else. But unfortunately time wasn't on our side, we would have liked to conduct a few more interviews. At one stage we did think he was going to confess and tell us what he knew. He did make one comment which he maintained he shouldn't have been asked without a solicitor present, which just wasn't the case at all.

"It's important to state that the question that was put to him, which he answered, was an open-ended question, it wasn't a 'yes' or 'no' response, it was a 'what do you know about …' question and his answer to that was very significant in that it corroborated exactly what the person who had come forward had said. It wasn't fed to him, it was an open-ended question and he just came out with something that literally coincided with what we had been told the week previous. I have to say it was quite chilling and I thought at that point in time, and my colleague who was with me thought the same, that he was going to come out with something at that point. But he didn't and just said he didn't want to be interviewed anymore. There was a nurse present at all times when he was being interviewed and we agreed that we would be guided by them as to how the questioning would continue. We were so close, yet so far."

Doyle said the woman who came forward, who was a survivor of the child molester, had nothing to gain by making the admissions as she bore no hatred towards the paedophile and had in fact forgiven him for his horrendous abuse towards her. "The person who came forward was very brave and courageous. I have a lot of respect for this person. I believe it took a lot of courage considering her own interaction with this particular man, I think she was remarkable. This woman told me she had found it in her heart to forgive this man. She had found religion through a family member and found it in her heart to forgive him so there was nothing for her to gain from coming forward. Her act was purely to see if she could assist with the investigation. And from the comments he made on his deathbed, they would only add further to her credibility."

Over the past 35 years, detectives working on the case have always made appeals to the public for their help. Doyle is of the strong belief that someone out there knows what happened to Philip that day and just needs them to come forward with that small missing piece of the jigsaw in order to solve the case.

"We did re-enactments and appealed to people on the anniversary of his disappearance over the years. There wasn't a single year that went by when we didn't appeal for people to come forward. All of this was done with the assistance of Philip's family who have been of huge help to us and who have been a huge assistance to me. Every person who came forward with potential information, we always discussed with the family. I kept in very close contact with them on a regular basis, updating them and asking them about certain individuals and would have been guided a lot about certain people by them."

Cooke was such a prolific abuser that the mere thought of one of his victims, while weak and frail on his deathbed, was enough to fill the dying paedophile with joy. Doyle said his twisted reaction was one which will remain with him for a long time.

"His recollection of a particular victim at one stage was such that he breathed very heavily while he recalled some of his interactions with this girl at the time. There was a sense of evil about it, there was a sense of macabre about it and there was definitely a sense that this guy had done this a lot more and was capable of a lot more."

Doyle believes there are people who possess the information which could solve the 35-year-old mystery and help bring Philip home to his family so they can give him a proper burial. And he said he would appeal to them to come forward and end their heartache and pain. "There are people out there that know. I'm obviously not in the force anymore but from knowing the way that An Garda Siochana operate I cannot see how any person who would come forward would be treated with anything other than the utmost dignity and respect. I would urge them to come forward and think of this as if it was your own family member. Philip is still a boy in the minds and hearts of his family, he's still a little boy who went missing and they just want to know where he is."

Philip's schoolbag holds the key, according to the former Detective Sergeant, as whoever dropped it back in the laneway could possess the vital information needed to solve the case. "The bag is huge because whoever put it there knows where it came from to be put there. The person who put the satchel there I believe has done nothing wrong, they haven't committed a crime, they could absolutely help solve this mystery. This one person just needs to come forward.

"There are so many people over the years who have probably not come forward with information, as they believed it was insignificant. They might have thought they were just doing a favour for someone they knew, or did it out of fear or out of even the promise of being brought somewhere for a McDonald's or something. What didn't seem big back then could be hugely significant now. Somebody with that information, if they came forward even on an anonymous basis initially or even sent an email to somebody they trusted, they could actually solve this crime, this mystery."

The retired detective said if Cooke was involved then hopefully someone who has information can now come forward in the knowledge that he is no longer a threat.

I believe there are a number of people who may possess vital information concerning Cooke and whether he was involved in Philip's disappearance. I know their identities but have so far not been able to track them down. I have forwarded all relevant information on to the authorities. Hopefully, one day someone will come forward with the information which will either conclusively determine whether Cooke was involved in Philip's abduction or not, but until that day comes, he will remain a person of interest.

# 12.

# Dead Ends

*'He walked into the room and just turned to me and said: "I have done terrible things Richie" … I know in my heart and soul what happened to Philip Cairns'*

In the days that followed Philip's disappearance, investigating officers would have interviewed and looked into well-known criminals and sex offenders who were living in and close to the Rathfarnham area. Every lead was followed up on and no stone was left unturned. One detective who worked on the case said there were numerous 'people of interest' during the initial stages of the investigation due to their criminal past. However, they were quickly eliminated from enquiries.

Retired cold case detective Alan Bailey said they thoroughly looked at potential suspects before ruling them out. "There was no certain person who we said, 'Oh, he was in the area or he could have been'." While former murder squad detective John Harrington said that during the early stages of the investigation there would have been a number of people who were deemed potential suspects in the case. "Everyone in the locality at the time would have been interviewed. There were several suspects but until proven guilty they are still innocent. I obviously can't say who they were. A suspect is a different thing to a guilty party."

To date, paedophile Eamon Cooke is the only person to be publicly named as a potential suspect. There is certainly circumstantial evidence which points towards the notorious child abuser, but no hard evidence. And while Cooke is still deemed a suspect, it's important to not pin the teenager's disappearance on him just in case he wasn't involved and the true culprit is still walking the streets. A detective told me: "It's important that Cooke's potential involvement is stringently investigated but it's also important to keep an open mind as it could be a case of someone local, who perhaps hasn't come across the Garda radar as yet or who is known but the missing piece of the jigsaw to tie them to the crime is missing."

There have been many reports of possible suspects or persons of interest over the years but none of them have ever come to fruition. In 1989, three years after Philip's disappearance, it was reported that gardaí from Tallaght were hoping to interview a local Rathfarnham man over the boy's suspected abduction. The *Sunday Tribune* stated that the man in question was identified by a mystery caller to the gardaí during a period of two months, involving four separate calls. Despite pleas by officers for the individual to get back in touch with them, he never did. Gardaí at the time said that none of the information could be verified and that it could have been merely a disgruntled person who had a grudge against a neighbour. However, one of the individuals mentioned by the man was allegedly someone who the gardaí had already noted as a possible suspect.

In 2007, it was reported in newspapers at the time that two women had come forward naming the same individual as a possible suspect following a fresh appeal by gardaí for information on the show Crimecall. One of the witnesses told gardaí that a man she was in a relationship with admitted knowing where the teenager was buried but said he would kill her if she went to the gardaí with the information. It was claimed in a report at the time that he had told her where Philip's remains were, but did not admit to killing him. However, Philip's father said at the time he had not been informed of such developments.

Officers are believed to have travelled to meet the man in question, who was no longer living in Ireland and had moved to another European country. But after conducting a lengthy interview with the individual, he was ruled out and the line of enquiry was closed.

The most recent report of another alleged suspect was in 2015 when gardener Richard Kavanagh came forward claiming his former employer was Philip's killer. His claims were reported in one of the national newspapers at the time. He was adamant at the time that a number of things led him to believe he was responsible for the teenager's disappearance and he said he had gone to the gardaí with the information he believed to be of importance.

When contacted, Mr Kavanagh told me that there were a number of incidents concerning his then employer which led him to believe the man, who we shall call 'John', was involved. He said his suspicions were initially raised when he was carrying out some maintenance work in the man's back garden in Rathfarnham and lost his footing and fell over a protruding piece of wood in the soil. He had spent hours that morning tidying up a large section of the garden before tripping over the foreign object. The owner of the property came running out to see what the commotion was. He was horrified when he saw the landscaper bending down to inspect what had caused his fall. He ran over and led the gardener inside. Mr Kavanagh, who lived a short distance away in Tallaght, thought no more of the incident in the garden until a short time later when 'John' approached him and blurted out something which stopped him in his tracks.

Mr Kavanagh met 'John' while out swimming at the Forty Foot in Sandycove, Co Dublin, during the mid-Eighties. He recalled the first time the pair met. "I did garden work and I still do garden maintenance. I used to swim in Sandycove in the Eighties and that is how I met 'John', at the Forty Foot. He came over to me one morning and asked me to hold on to some jewellery for him while he swam. In 1989 he asked me to cut a bit of a hedge for him and take some rubbish out of his house. I then used to go and cut the grass for him. I would go and do it and get out of there quickly. He was an odd guy. The first time I went to the house he opened the door and he had no clothes on, nothing whatsoever. I told him to put some clothes on. He went and got dressed and I went and did the back garden."

He said he first became suspicious of 'John' following the incident in his back garden. "The years went by and one day I was in the back garden. I was picking up a few plums from the tree he had down the back and I just chipped my toe on some timber, it was like the lid of a coffin. I tripped over it and managed to catch myself on the wall. I pulled it up and he came out to the back garden and was shaking. There was definitely something there. I remember thinking he had a dog and had buried it. I actually thought to myself, 'I wonder what he has buried under there'. He used to be always peeping out the window at me doing work in the garden."

Mr Kavanagh said one afternoon while he was putting some tiles up in the man's bathroom, 'John' approached him and blurted out a very unusual statement which would stick with the 70-year-old for years to come. "I was putting two tiles on the bathroom wall for him and he came out all dressed up – spotless, shaven and looking good, which was not him as he always looked a bit dirty. He walked into the room and just turned to me and said: 'I have done terrible things, Richie'. I just looked at him as if to say,'What did you do?' I can't remember much after that as I just wanted to get out of there."

And he claims 'John' reiterated the statement years later when the two men bumped into each other. "The last time I saw him he said again, 'Richie, remember the day I told you I did terrible things?' I never asked him about what he meant, I'm sick as a dog now for not."

Mr Kavanagh also recalled how he believes the man in question may have tried to drug him. The individual, who was not known to gardaí, offered him a drink while carrying out hard manual work. Mr Kavanagh said after just one sip he started to feel dizzy. "It was definitely spiked, without a doubt. The room was spinning after I took a sip. Every time after that he would try and give me a drink but I always brought my own stuff. I never felt really comfortable with him. I didn't dislike him but I wouldn't have trusted him and he had a weird way of going on."

It would only be years later when reading up about the schoolboy's disappearance that Mr Kavanagh said he started piecing memories together. As well as the unusual activities in 'John's' back garden, he realised that there may have been a connection to Philip and the Cairns family. The family man says 'John', who has since died, drove a similar Red Japanese car to the one which formed part of the early Garda investigation into Philip's disappearance and sold it a short time after the teenager went missing. "He drove a red Japanese car in 1986. I only saw the car once, I was told it was sold to buy a motorbike. I never saw the car again. Why did he get rid of the car?"

And he said 'John' lived close to where the missing teenager's satchel schoolbag was found and also claims he was a member of the Dublin Sea Anglers Club, which Philip and his father were avid members of. He said he was also extremely religious and would have attended local prayer meetings regularly, like the Cairns family. "He used to make all the flies for fly fishing. Every time I was there he was making them. 'John' went to local prayer meetings too like the Cairns family. He used to give me little prayer cards."

Mr Kavanagh said the man in question even helped to look for the teenager following his disappearance in 1986. "He was also involved in the search for Philip. There are video clips out there, which I have seen, of him taking part at that time."

After playing on his mind for years he went to detectives in 2010 and made a statement about what he knew and believed had happened. He urged officers at Tallaght Garda Station to dig up the garden of the property in south Dublin. "I first made a statement to the guards in 2010. I then made a further two in 2011. Two detectives came to my house and spent three hours talking to me. I told them exactly what I knew and where the house was. They showed me a picture of 'John' and asked me if it was him. I knew in my heart what he was capable of doing. The age, the description, he would have been in his 50s at the time Philip disappeared, the same description as the man who was spotted with a schoolboy, possibly Philip, at the time."

Mr Kavanagh is adamant 'John' had a role to play in Philip's disappearance and believes the teen's body is still buried in the back garden of the property. He said he would like to appeal to the homeowners directly to excavate the small patch of ground in order to determine once and for all if his beliefs are true or not.

He also claims to have spoken to Philip's mother on a number of occasions to try to convince her of what he believes. "I know in my heart and soul what happened to Philip Cairns. I have spoken to the Cairns family about this. I have spoken to Mrs Cairns four times, going back to 2010. I met her late last year too and was at her house and spoke to her. She asked me exactly where the house was and I told her. I think she believes everything I have said.

"Everything I have said is the truth, I had no reason to go to Mrs Cairns' house. We talked at the front door and I just told her what I believed, that Philip was buried in the back garden of that house. The truth will come out, I believe in the truth and that's what has kept me going. I have no reason to be making any of this up. I still think Philip is in that back garden now. I know in my heart and soul what was in that garden." He concluded: "I believe 'John' brought Philip back to the house that day and that was the last of him."

According to one detective I talked to, the man in question was looked into but there was nothing to merit further investigation. There was unfortunately no hard evidence to back up the claims being made.

Up until this point in the investigation there is still only one individual who is deemed a potential suspect – Eamon Cooke. One detective told me: "He is in my eyes the number one suspect at this moment in time and until someone can prove otherwise he remains in my view the most plausible person of interest."

# 13.

# Gates Of Hell

*'Philip's abductor may have ticked all and every box for the personality disorder of them all – anti-social personality disorder – or psychopathy as it's more commonly known'*

Many people will have only seen or heard of criminal profiling or forensic psychology from popular TV shows like Criminal Minds and Cracker. But throughout the world, law enforcement agencies, including the FBI and CIA in America and the Metropolitan Police in England, call on forensic psychologists for their expertise. They are called in to help identify the likely personality and behavioural characteristics of the offender following close analysis of the evidence in the case.

Investigators have also been known to use forensic psychologists or criminologists to help them narrow down their number of suspects or to give advice on how best to interrogate a suspect who is already in custody. In Ireland, An Garda Siochana do not routinely use criminal psychologists in ongoing criminal cases or Serious Crime Review Team investigations.

The first well-known case of a criminal profiler being called in to assist police officers occurred in 1956 in New York. Frustrated investigators called on psychiatrist James Brussel, who was then New York State's assistant commissioner of mental hygiene, to examine crime scenes and notes which had been left by someone who terrorised the city by planting 33 bombs and had managed to evade capture for 16 years. After exhausting every other avenue they called on Mr Brussel for his help.

Through careful examination and analysis, he was able to build a picture of the possible culprit. He was able to ascertain that the suspect, among other things, was of foreign descent, self-educated and in his 50s. His remarkable techniques helped officers to track down George Metesky, who was known as the "mad bomber". He had planted the devices around New York, including in phone boxes and packed cinemas, each one more powerful than the last. Although his explosives did not kill anybody, they left many victims seriously injured. Had it not been for Mr Brussel's profiling, he may never have been caught.

The use of a criminal psychologist could prove highly beneficial in many unsolved Irish cases of abduction and murder, including that of missing Philip Cairns, a number of former detectives who worked on the investigation have said. One officer who worked on the teenager's suspected abduction said it could help to build a picture of who the perpetrator might be. It may also help to establish whether Philip, who was a well-behaved boy, was likely to have got into a stranger's car and, if so, how he may have been coaxed to do so. Or it could provide clues to suggest that it was someone known to him or even, as has been discussed, a pillar of society?

I decided to call on two top experts in this field for their thoughts on the case. Top British forensic physiologist Dr Julian Boon believes gardaí should investigate paedophile Eamon Cooke further and dig up his land, especially the site he owned in Stepaside. After looking at the case in depth, Dr Boon said: "It doesn't matter that the tank up the mountains (which Cooke had) is now empty underground, modern-day forensic techniques could very well prove helpful. It should be properly forensically investigated. Why the bloody hell would he have such a cave? I'm reminded of a case about Leonard Lake and his Chinese accomplice in America where he had an underground place. It would give you nightmares what those two got up to."

Dr Boon, who helped authorities with cases including the Harold Shipman trial in 1999, became known in the UK as 'the real-life Cracker'. After spending some time examining the Philip Cairns case, he said that Cooke was a master manipulator and smart operator so may have got rid of any forensic evidence if he was involved. Despite that, he would still put him at the top of the list of possible suspects in Philip's abduction due to his background, personality and the crimes he had previously committed.

"Eamon Cooke has to be at the front. The problem we have is that Cooke, by anyone's standards, was a slippery customer in his day and was very careful. Notice the children who he took polaroid pictures of, the whole thing is very, very careful and what we would call 'forensically aware' for his day. So who is to say there hasn't been other cases? Maybe not where the child has gone completely missing but if you are threatened that, 'You do this and I'm going to put pictures up of you in the bus stop, at the train station so everyone can see what you have been doing. That's a pretty powerful means by which to control people and children in particular. What nobody is in doubt about is that Cooke was a pervert and horrible individual, psychopathic as hell in his complete disregard of children."

There are three types of paedophiles according to Dr Boon, who has come face to face with some of the most notorious murderers, rapists and paedophiles over the course of his 30-plus-year career. "One of the things that I always give lectures on when it comes to covering paedophilia, is can they be changed? Can they be rewired through therapy? To which, you can have my view, no they cannot. All you can do is stop them doing it, not stop them wanting to do it.

"If you are going to believe a sex offender's treatment programme can make any difference whatsoever, you have three potential outcomes.

"One is that they are highly intelligent, the paedophiles, which would appear to be this man's (Cooke's) saving grace. I hate to say – and they get very clever at manipulating the children and not leaving a trail – but they will continue to do it.

"Two, they are as thick as two planks, in which case they will, as I have had repeated to me, say: 'I'm sorry Julian. I didn't mean to. I promise I will never do it again,' and you know

damn well that the next time they are down the park and they
see a little boy or a little girl going into the loos that the lust will
overcome them and all their promises will just evaporate there
and then. The only people you can get through to, but not stop
the desire for paedophilic activity, are the (third kind) using the
technique: 'Go within 200 yards of the school and we will have
you,' and that works."

Meanwhile, Irish criminologist and lecturer in Forensic
Psychology, Professor John O'Keeffe, said profiling a possible
suspect could prove very beneficial to the investigation. He
explained how building a picture of the person responsible
could help detectives. "It is invaluable to try to understand
the personality type of offenders – as well, of course, as their
social, familial and environmental background.

"The bigger the picture you create here, the more likely it
is you may be able to narrow down your search. For example,
those with psychopathic personalities behave in very distinct
criminal ways to non-psychopathic criminals. Creating a
personality sketch from those who may have known an offender
may take you into their very soul and so their motivations –
which can be very different to those, for example, with other
personality types. Get to know their motives and their modus
and you are halfway there."

The well-known criminologist said, despite the very small
amount of evidence in Philip's case, it was still possible to build
a profile of the person responsible for his alleged kidnapping.
"In a case like the disappearance of Philip Cairns, it can be
invaluable. We have to do the impossible. From the available
evidence we need to step into the shoes of someone who
potentially has no remorse or empathy for any living creature;

who will stop at nothing to satisfy their own internal cravings; who will cross every Rubicon where you and I would halt; a man who, 'knows the words but doesn't know the music'; whom has only proto-emotions; who is effectively sub-human, albeit in human form. Walking into those hellish shoes may be impossible for many. But until we do, we may never find the answer as to why Philip Cairns was taken during the middle of that fateful day of the 23rd October 1986."

Prof O'Keeffe said it's highly unlikely Philip would have willingly got into a car with someone he didn't know or recognise. He said in the Eighties that 'stranger danger' was very prominent and kids were regularly warned not to go off with people who were not known to them. If Philip was abducted by an unknown person, the likelihood is that someone would have heard his screams or seen the commotion on the busy Dublin road. The criminologist said it is important to put the year in which Philip disappeared into context.

"In order to properly consider whether Philip was the type of boy that might have taken a lift from someone he knew or did not know, it is important to firstly consider the era in which the abduction occurred. The 1980s in Ireland were marked by the emergence of what we know in criminology as, 'Folk Devils' creating 'Moral Panics'.

"If a generalised heinous type could be portrayed by the media in a few words, it would. Crime, particularly sexual crime, was not nuanced. Bad men in grubby macs stood behind bushes waiting to "flash" at any given opportunity – especially at young people and women. Sex offences were committed outside the home, not in it. Period.

"While there was a curious tolerance of sexual innuendo

in the media that we would not recognise today, this was juxtaposed with the fear of 'stranger danger'. In other words, all crime, especially crime against children, was considered to emanate from strangers, not family or friends. This of course we now know to be categorically not the case, quite the opposite, but in the dreary, economic and social gloom of 1980s Ireland, all supposed truths – albeit without any basis in fact – were clung to like life-preservers."

For these reasons, Prof O'Keeffe said, it's very unlikely the teen would have willingly just got into a car with someone who he didn't know. "Philip therefore, like all young boys of his age, would have been ultra aware of 'stranger danger' not the familial type. While it is true that 'hitch-hiking' and 'thumbing lifts' was common at the time, it was not so popular in urban areas. It is therefore unlikely that he would have willingly, with no coaxing, gotten into the car of a stranger. Someone known to him most certainly – a stranger, far less likely."

Due to Philip being a very well-behaved teenager, even if he did not want to get into the car of someone he knew, he might have found it hard to say no to them. "The fact that he was quiet and well-mannered will have ensured he probably never would have said a robust 'no' to an adult he knew."

And when it comes to who would have carried out such a daring abduction in the middle of the day on a very busy Dublin Road, Prof O'Keefe said it was most likely someone who had an anti-social or narcissistic personality disorder.

What would have been deemed acceptable behaviour towards a child in public in 1986 would not be seen in the same way now. "Adult behaviour towards children in public was very different to that of today. Today, no adult would randomly put his arm around a child in the street whom he did not know, or make any type of adult remark to them.

"The Eighties were different and boundaries were blurred. Sex offenders hid in full view and fooled all around them while other adults appeared indifferent to what society would now view as inappropriate physical contact and general conservation. Having said that, it seems likely that Philip's abductor will have been one who possibly had anti-social, or perhaps its lesser cousin, narcissistic personality disorder. These personalities are evidenced by certain, very specific behaviours. Narcissism, glib yet superficially charming; a comically grandiose sense of self-worth, manipulation in discussion and an utter lack of remorse, guilt or empathy.

"Couple this with a likely impulsivity, poor behavioural controls and an excessive need for stimulation, and Philip's abductor may have ticked all and every box for the personality disorder of them all – anti-social personality disorder – or psychopathy as it is more commonly known. We also have to accept the possibility, however, that Philip's abductor was living in a time when simple requests to jump in a car and 'come for a spin' were not viewed with suspicion. However, on balance it seems very unlikely that Philip's abductor did not evidence some, if not all of these personality flaws."

As we know, prolific paedophile Eamon Cooke became a person of interest in 2016 when one of his victims claimed to have witnessed the serial child abuser assault Philip at his Dublin radio station. There are people who believe that Cooke, despite being a paedophile who would have abused any child who came within a foot of him, was not capable of murder. But there are many, including detectives who worked on the investigation, who believe the monster was a violent individual who, if provoked, was more than capable of killing somebody.

So does Prof O'Keeffe believe that Cooke fits the criminal profile of someone who was capable of carrying out such a heinous act?

"Certainly. From those who knew him, he has been variously described as a 'vile, evil, violent, psychopathic individual' who, if he did not kill, was certainly capable of killing. He was also a paedophile, which would of course put him firmly in the frame in this case. 'Paedophiles' are those who abuse pre-pubescent children. 'Hebephiles' abuse only underage post-pubescent children. Many child sex offenders will, of course, abuse across the childhood range and only opportunity will tend to stand in their way. Many hebephiles – and those who abuse children of all ages – will often have psychopathic personality traits and be what is known as a 'Hare Psychopath'. The profile of Eamon Cooke alone may suggest he is a prime suspect in the disappearance of Philip Cairns. He will not, at any moment in the abduction, have had a scintilla of conscience or remorse for what he had done, or was about to do with Philip. He is, to quote the world expert on psychopathy, Robert Hare, entirely a man without conscience. Aside from circumstantial and direct evidence, it is this profile that additionally puts him firmly in the picture in relation to Philip's disappearance."

Cooke was a serial child abuser and was known to verbally and physically abuse those around him. But do these personality characteristics lend themselves to someone who is able to carry out murder?

Since his long history of violence has come to light, many believe the circumstances surrounding his first wife's death should also be re-examined. She died of a suspected heart attack but now many people who knew Cooke believe he may have had a role to play in her premature death. As well as this, he was also involved in a fire bombing incident and blew up a monument at the age of 12. So he had a tendency for violence, but does that make him capable of murder? Prof O'Keefe believes it to certainly be the case.

"Eamon Cooke's personality and past says more than we need to know about his capabilities when it comes to taking lives. A psychopath is only as 'good' as his heinous acts and in this regard Cooke failed to disappoint. Psychopathic personality traits? Tick box. Child abuser? Tick box. Random, capricious violence? Tick box. Grave suspicion as to the circumstances surrounding his wife's death? Tick box. Psychopaths and narcissists such as Cooke will display higher and lower levels of different psychopathic traits. Think of it like a sound desk. Some score lower on, for example, lack of remorse but higher on violence. Others will achieve high scores on grandiose behaviours, others on manipulation."

So Cooke was more than capable of carrying out a murder and in fact hit a lot of the markers which would place his as a very plausible suspect. "By all reports, Cooke scored high on all – especially what some psychopaths will consider 'recreational violence'.

"Everyone reports being fearful of Cooke – not just children. Cooke was the master not just of violence – as we saw when he petrol bombed a house – but, just as importantly, the threat of violence was there. That was arguably a far greater weapon in his predator armoury."

Cooke was a household name due to his popular station

Radio Dublin so even if Philip didn't know the well-known Dublin personality he may have recognised him from being in the newspapers and being on the radio. Or perhaps, if Philip spotted young kids in the car with Cooke, he felt less threatened. Prof O'Keefe said most predators who carry out abductions tend to stick to areas they know as they feel comfortable in their surroundings and can also escape quickly if necessary.

"As a general proposition, criminals, at all levels, don't travel. They don't like to − it takes them out of their comfort zone. Someone from inner-city Dublin will be much more comfortable perpetrating a burglary on a neighbour's house than one in Foxrock − though arguably the rewards would be greater there. This is known as 'distance decay'. Similarly, when it comes to sexual crimes, child sex offenders will often go where there is an opportunity and they may be happier when that opportunity is relatively local − both in the metaphorical and literal sense."

Paedophiles are even more inclined to commit their crimes in areas which are known to them as they believe they blend in and therefore stand less of a chance of being recognised and caught out, Prof O'Keeffe added. "One caveat − child sex offenders of a certain type are also known to travel more than other criminals to avoid detection.

"Cooke may not have been one of these, however − one of many sex offenders of his generation to simply 'hide in full view'. Remember, in 1986, there was no Sat Nav, no Google Maps, no mobile phones. You either knew your way around your locality or you did not. Local areas such as Ballyroan could contain a complex enough level of streets, roads, estates and lanes − to those who were not familiar.

"Furthermore, whoever abducted Philip, would have needed to know their exit and know it fairly quickly. If you have committed a crime such as this one, you do not want to be wandering around streets you do not know with your victim." But he added: "The likelihood is that even if the offender was not local, he knew the area very well − or alternatively was so blinded by his own grandiose sense of self-worth, that the possibility of getting lost did not even cross his mind.

"Whoever abducted Philip Cairns was standing at the gates of hell. It is difficult to imagine that any version of God would not have now banished such an individual to the Lake of Torment."

# 14.

# Closure

*'I would love to see him again ...*
*I know deep down that the possibility*
*is remote. You have to hope for the best*
*and prepare for the worst. More than*
*likely there won't be a happy ending'*

Despite the long passage of time since Philip was reported missing, the case remains open and the investigation into his disappearance is still very much live. Although he is deemed by many as having been abducted and sadly killed, his case is still that of a missing person and not a murder investigation. Until his remains are recovered or there is substantial evidence to back up this unfortunate turn of events, the case will stay in the missing persons category.

While still holding out hope that he is alive, Philip's own family sadly fear the worst. All they want now is to be able to bring his remains home so they can give him a proper burial. His sister Mary echoed these thoughts and said more than anything they would like to have a grave where their elderly mother Alice, who still lives at the family home on Ballyroan Road, can visit. "We would really like to bring Philip home, give him a burial and somewhere for our mother to go where she knows where he is. It would be just for her to be able to say goodbye to Philip, in the way she would like to know what happened to him. I mean, your life moves forward in some respects but then there is just this part of our life that has stood still," she said in 2020.

The investigation into Philip's disappearance has never stopped. From time to time, there are developments that raise hope or prompt completely new lines of enquiry. Eight years after Philip's abduction, in 1994, detectives received an anonymous letter which claimed the teenager was involved in a tragic accident. The suggestion threw a curve ball at investigating officers who had always assumed he had been abducted. The letter received by officers stated that a boy fitting Philip's description had been seen walking behind three other lads at a bridge over the nearby Dodder River, from Dodder Road to Bushy Park, close to his home. Gardaí wanted to explore the claims and in order to determine their validity decided to make a public appeal for any further information on this possible scenario during a televised update on the case.

Detective Joe Costello told viewers of RTÉ's Crimeline programme how, "Hurricane Charley had struck in August of that year, and this particular bridge had been damaged as a result of the hurricane." He said there was the possibility that Philip and some friends may have taken the day off to go to the Dodder, which was most likely flooded, and there was a possibility that "an accident had ensued". He appealed for the author of the letter they had received, as well as anyone else who may have been in the area on the day and had seen this particular event, to come forward. Despite the plea, there were no further witnesses to such a scenario and the lead went cold. It is believed gardaí ruled out the theory as there was no evidence to suggest this incident actually took place and Philip was not the kind of teen who would have deliberately missed school.

In a new revelation, former Detective Inspector Gerry O'Carroll said there was also another occasion during the course of the investigation which he regrets not looking at in further detail. He said it has been playing on his mind for the last number of years after initially paying it very little attention at the time.

It centres on a well-known Dublin criminal who claimed during a Garda interview to him in 1995 that he knew who had murdered Philip. The convicted offender said it was a religious Brother he knew who had abducted and killed the schoolboy. The well-known criminal told O'Carroll that he was having a sexual relationship with the Brother, who had allegedly made the shocking admission to him.

O'Carroll said the Dublin criminal rang Sundrive Garda Station to report a (decoy) crime in order to be brought into custody along with the alleged suspect so that the information about Philip could be divulged to officers.

Recalling the incident, O'Carroll told me: "You are hearing this for the first time. When I was at Sundrive Road, we got a phone call that there was a man with a gun in a pub.

"So I got a team of men, because the caller said, 'You will recognise this man and he's with another man, he's wearing this coat and this shirt'.

"We went in and pounced, guns drawn. We brought the two of them down to the station. One of the guys who we arrested had a load of ammunition in his pocket, .45 calibre. This guy – who was a criminal from Crumlin – said he had made the call on purpose … I think he had a bit of a brain injury or something, he wasn't right in the head. When I interviewed him, he said, 'Brother – I'm telling ya, he killed Philip Cairns'. It would have been 1995, or around then. It came out of the blue. He said he had put in the call so that we could arrest the fella. I went in and interviewed this other guy."

But O'Carroll said despite his best efforts he failed to get any more information out of the Brother regarding the shocking accusation. "I interrogated him for four hours. He was evasive. Horrible. Very argumentative. I said to him, 'What about Philip Cairns?' and he said, 'I don't know anything about that'. I don't think he was based down there (where Philip lived) but called down occasionally. It happened at 8pm and I was still interviewing this Brother at four o'clock in the morning. Eventually, he said he had nothing to do with it.

"The Brother is now dead. I never went to his Order or anything. I didn't do enough, I suppose. I was too busy in my own field. I probably should have done more. I was busy enough in Sundrive Road, I had armed robberies and murders of my own. I did what I could, I spent hours with the man. I never forgot about him."

The public have always been fascinated by Philip's case and, over the years, many people have come forward offering to help in whatever way they possibly could. One particular incident which sticks out was in January 1995 when lottery winner James Connolly offered a substantial reward of £20,000 to help solve the case.

At the time, the father-of-ten said he was glad to be in a position to help out. He had won £250,000 on the 'spin the wheel' lottery game and Philip's case had always fascinated him. He said at the time how he wanted to use the money to help solve the investigation. "This is not a goodwill gesture on my part, it is done to tempt someone out who hasn't been out before. I have been studying this for the last three years and I believe I have information that links everything together – it is like a jigsaw and all I need is the last piece to say 'that is it' and that is why I am putting up the £20,000.

"I would appeal to them not to carry this terrible secret to the grave. I appeal at this time especially to the friends and former classmates of Philip who might have information. A lot of people remember where they were the day John F. Kennedy was shot – well, I have the same thing about the day Philip Cairns disappeared."

The street trader, who sold sweets and chocolate at a pitch beside the Halfpenny Bridge in Dublin city centre every Sunday morning, said the reward was for anyone who could offer information leading to the "apprehension and conviction of the person or persons responsible." The teenager's father, Philip Snr, welcomed the donation.

However, tragedy would strike the generous man and his family just months later in July, when along with his wife Bridie they were involved in a serious car accident. The couple were travelling on the Navan Road when they crashed into another vehicle outside Dunshaughlin, Co Meath. Mrs Connolly died from her injuries and Mr Connolly and one of his daughters were left critically injured.

Another financial incentive to solve the case came in 2007. Crimestoppers, a joint initiative between An Garda Siochana and the business community, offered €10,000 to anyone who would come forward with important information. Those who might have information about Philip's disappearance were asked to call the freephone number anonymously. But unfortunately, despite the financial incentive, like every previous year, no new leads emerged.

Officers investigating the case have never allowed the story to go silent, always keeping it in the national consciousness, appealing for information in the hope that one day it will lead to them getting the breakthrough they need.

Another unexpected development in the case came when gardaí carried out two searches, 50 metres apart, on a quarter acre of land off Whitechurch Road in Rathfarnham, close to the M50 – again acting on information from the public.

An elderly woman had come forward claiming she had seen a grave-shaped mound, at the now overgrown site, around the time the teenager went missing. Detectives decided to take no chances and started a detailed search of the location in which the woman claimed to have seen the soil disturbance. Members of the Garda Technical Bureau carried out a fingertip examination and also used specialist equipment which looked at soil disturbance. Specialist equipment was brought in to help with the dig which showed there had been some displacement of soil but no remains were unearthed.

Retired Detective Sergeant Doyle said the search in 2009

was just one of many his team conducted over the years. "We searched the Grange Golf Club. A lady had come forward and she had seen something at the time and she felt something was buried there. She saw the particular person who buried it and we got geophysics involved and they came up and shot X-rays through the soil.

"They found what would be regarded as dislodgement of ground which would be consistent with a grave being dug. There was evidence of soil displacement at the time. We dug it but we found nothing. We extended it out to a second area of soil. But unfortunately there was nothing there either."

Doyle said that while in charge of the investigation, he co-ordinated many excavations of land in the hope that one of them would lead to Philip's remains finally being found. And there were no shortcuts when it came to the searches, with the most state-of-the-art technology being used every time.

There were also many searches which were carried out without the public's knowledge. Recalling one such dig, Doyle revealed: "When I was involved in the case I searched the back of an old local mill that they used to clean the wool from sheep. Information came our way that he might have been buried there. We got in for a weekend, nobody knew about it, with diggers and excavated the whole area. We had a forensic archaeologist with us just in case we found something. But unfortunately we found nothing."

Like others, former Detective Sergeant Doyle personally believes that there may be someone out there who holds the missing piece of the puzzle which could finally help solve the case. "The public have always responded at difficult times … thousands of statements have been taken, numerous searches carried out and re-enactments aired on TV to prompt further awareness in the hope of a breakthrough."

Making a further appeal, he said: "Perhaps you were a child, a young person or a teenager in 1986. Perhaps you heard or saw something that at the time seemed innocent or you were simply too scared to speak about it. With the passage of time you may now see things differently and you are no longer scared to speak up. Perhaps it is time to free yourself of the burden of that secret and speak of what you know.

"I am an ex-member of An Garda Siochana and I have worked on the investigation. Please do not let fear, guilt or shame stop you from doing the right thing now. You will not be judged. I have no doubt that you will be treated with courtesy, dignity and respect. Your call could make the difference and bring peace to Philip's family."

Another journalist who is close to Philip's story is Conor Feehan from the *Irish Independent*. Conor, who grew up just down the road from Philip, remembers the day he heard about the teenager's disappearance. Feehan, who would have been finishing up at Colaiste Eanna as the teenager started it, said it was a very sad story which shocked the whole neighbourhood at the time. Recalling the day in question, he told me: "The first I knew that Philip Cairns had gone missing was when my family were having dinner in our busy home in Rathfarnham. My younger sister told us the brother of a girl in her class had not come home the day before, and her family were worried about him. I suppose at the time we thought he'd turn up and there would be some sort of story that would explain it all, and life would return to normal. Philip never turned up, and life never returned to normal for his family, or for Rathfarnham. I had gone to Colaiste Eanna, the same school Philip had started in that September in 1986. In fact, I had just done the Leaving Cert there, so as I was leaving he was starting in first year."

Feehan said it was extremely uncommon for a child to go missing at the time, especially from a quiet, leafy suburb like Rathfarnham. "It was unheard of for kids to go missing in 1986, especially lads as young as Philip, and when another day went by without a sign of him people really started to worry. The 'Have You Seen This Boy' notices went up in the local shops, and it was strange to see your home suburb on the news and being written about in newspapers. Then, six days after he went missing, Philip's schoolbag was found dumped in a local laneway that had already been searched, and the mystery into his disappearance grew deeper and even more sinister. There was a sense of panic in the community. It was late October and searches were marred by bad weather and a lack of daylight. It would be years later that I would start writing about Philip's disappearance as a reporter, coming to journalism in 1999 more than 10 years after he vanished."

Feehan said there had been many theories locally over the years as to what happened to the teenager. "One thing I learned quickly in the reporting world is that in the absence of information you get speculation, and speculation has a way of growing roots and branches and becoming part of the landscape. Had Philip run away? Had he been abducted? Everyone had questions, but nobody had any answers, so speculation and theories thrived."

The reporter recalled how surreal it was writing about the teenager's case. "One of the first times I wrote about Philip's disappearance was after the *Sunday Independent* ran a story in 2002 that the young schoolboy was murdered and buried in the grounds of Loreto Abbey in Rathfarnham, according to information it had received and passed on to gardaí. The land had been developed since, and the story never yielded anything.

"Another time I was reporting on the story was when a dig was carried out on grounds in the Whitechurch area of Rathfarnham, at the foothills of the Dublin Mountains. Gardaí, acting on information they had received following one of many appeals, had ground in the church surveyed, and an anomaly was found under the surface. But it turned out to be a large stone. Then in 2016 it emerged that people were nominating convicted paedophile and radio station owner Eamon Cooke with Philip's disappearance. I remember calling to see Philip's mother, Alice, and asking her about these claims, and she said Philip had never known Cooke or ever talked about him."

Like many of the officers who have worked on the case over the years, Feehan is also of the belief that the schoolboy's bag could hold the key to solving the mystery. "It sounds childish, but if only that schoolbag could talk. Still wrapped in plastic to protect it forensically, it looked like the bag we all had as kids in the 1980s. A simple canvas bag bought in an army surplus shop on Capel Street, with a shoulder strap and a flap that closed it with two fastening straps.

"Being made of canvas, you could write or draw on it with biro, and band names would often be written on them by young lads to personalise them. Philip had done the same to his one. Seeing the bag made me feel sad, frustrated, and angry.

"As part of that story I went back to Alice and asked her about the bag. She told me she frequently uses the long narrow concrete laneway where his schoolbag was found, often on her way to Ballyroan church to pray for him. 'I always look down at the spot beside the lamppost where his bag was left, and I always wonder. It's very sad,' she said.

"As a local, and somebody who has interviewed Philip's family and gardaí, have I any insights into the case? Sadly, no. It's more than 30 years ago now, but I feel that if the case had happened today it would stand a better chance of being solved."

Feehan, having grown up in the area and knowing the little laneways and roads like the back of his hand, is of the belief that Philip wasn't grabbed off the side of the road. "For what it's worth, and my 'speculation' is as valid and invalid as anyone else's, I don't think Philip was grabbed off the street and bundled into a car. Ballyroan Road is too busy, and at that time there would have been scores of kids returning to school after lunch. I think that Philip was approached, called, or coerced by someone he knew and trusted, and something either pre-planned or spur-of-the-moment happened. I think there are people who know what happened, and maybe through fear they still carry that with them. I hope someday the reality of what happened becomes known and Philip is found."

The disappearance of Philip Cairns has remained one of the most baffling and mysterious cases the gardaí have ever encountered. Also known by officers as case number IRGSmk5, for the past 35 years detectives have worked tirelessly to try to establish what happened to the teenager on the day he went missing. Despite there being a number of leads and new lines of enquiry, no information has led to officers finding out categorically what happened to Philip that day.

The massive amount of work and man hours during the early stages of the investigation is evident in the fact that a staggering 1,220 angles or lines of enquiry were followed up on in the first year alone. And a further 370 police statements were lodged. More than 200 reported sightings of Philip were also followed up on by officers but sadly none of them ever came to fruition. Nobody has ever been arrested for Philip's abduction, however I have heard from one detective that officers were "extremely close" to it at one stage.

The lengthy investigation has left its mark not just on those who are currently working on the case but also on the many now retired detectives. Former cop O'Carroll said it's a case he has never forgotten, so much so he still keeps a picture of the young schoolboy in his home.

"I have been plagued by this case. I can remember every tiny detail. A lot of colleagues are dead and gone but this case remains with me. So much so that I have always kept a picture of this young boy. He's in my mind's eye in his school uniform and I still have his picture in my bedroom. It has always resonated with me because I had boys of the same age and I was living not too far away. I lived in Rathfarnham, in Moyville, and Ballyroan was only a mile away and my kids were going to go to that school. My grandson attends there now. It's one of the few cases that is still so fresh in my memory. I have never forgotten Philip Cairns."

He said what struck him in regards to Philip's case is that apart from parental kidnappings, very few children have been randomly abducted off the side of the road in Ireland never to be seen again. "We don't have milk cartons like in America (the cartons were used to publicise cases of missing children during the Eighties and Nineties) where thousands of children go missing every year. Mary Boyle and Philip Cairns are the only two children in the last 100 years. That's why it created such public interest, undying interest really, because everyone remembers the day Philip disappeared. I have thought about this for 35 years, I have gone over every possible scenario on Earth."

Former Detective Sergeant Tom Doyle still hopes the mystery of Philip's disappearance can be explained. He said cases can be solved even after a long period of time and referred to the case of convicted killer John Crerar. The army sergeant was caught and convicted for the brutal murder of Kildare woman Phyllis Murphy almost 23 years after he killed her. A detective involved in the case at the time kept a blood sample collected years earlier and, as DNA testing techniques advanced, he decided to have it tested once more.

He urged anyone who may have been forced to take part in the abduction or leave the schoolbag in the laneway, who was possibly a juvenile at the time, to not be afraid in coming forward. "You may not be directly responsible for Philip's disappearance. You may have been told or coerced into putting the bag there and now fear you could be held responsible for his disappearance because of that. If someone had control or influence over you back in 1986 you would be older and wiser now, and know that doing the right thing is the most important thing. It's never too late, I can't stress that enough."

But it is, of course, Philip's family who have suffered the most pain since their loved one vanished. Despite the long passage of time they are none the wiser as to what happened to him that day.

In recent years, gardaí have issued a computer-generated photograph of what Philip might have looked like at the age of 21. Officers gathered up and forwarded on pictures of Philip, his parents, his four sisters and brother to a company in America who used them to generate a new updated image using their computer photo-ageing process.

The childhood picture of Philip had been replaced with an image of a handsome young man and, in a bittersweet moment, his parents got to see what their missing son would look like if he was still around. The only common similarity between old photos of him and the new picture was his tell-tale smile.

No doubt the hardest struggle for Philip's family is not knowing if he is still alive or dead. His brother and best friend, Eoin, said he would like to still believe he is alive but following such a long passage of time it is highly unlikely.

"I'd like to think that he would just return to us," he told Ryan Tubridy on RTÉ Radio One. "My mam obviously hopes that he will return to us, but really, after 29 years, more than likely the thinking is that we would just like to know where he is, where he remains really.

"If he is alive, I hope he's well. I would love if he'd contact us and let us know he's well. I would love to see him again, of course. I know really, deep down, that the likelihood of it, the possibility, is very remote. You have to hope for the best and prepare for the worst. More than likely there won't be a happy ending. After 29 years, we just want an ending. It is still an open investigation and every couple of years, we sit down with the guards to see if there are any new developments. The guards have been fantastic."

Talking to me in 2021, it was clear that the family retain special memories of the son and brother who has left such a gap in their lives over the past 35 years. They remain as they have been throughout − dignified and quietly determined to finally find some answers.

In a statement they gave to me for this book, they said: "Philip was a happy, warm and caring young boy who was dearly loved. We feel his loss every day and he is always in our hearts and thoughts. We appreciate all the support we have received over the years and appeal again to anyone who may have information to please contact the gardaí."

They say losing a child brings the greatest sadness of all and not a day goes by that Philip's heartbroken mother doesn't think of her lost little boy.

Along with her late husband Philip Snr, she has lived through every parent's worst nightmare and yet shown the resilience that has provided an inspiration to others. Her continuing hope is that there will be a final chapter which brings the family peace. "Somebody out there knows what happened to my son and I wish that they would just have the courage to come forward and tell us."

# Acknowledgements

I would firstly like to extend my thoughts to the Cairns family, who have had to endure pain no family should have to. Their strength in such heartbreaking circumstances, which has never waivered, truly shows their determination to find out what happened to their loved one. I really hope that one day they get to bring Philip home.

To Dermot Browne, who helps so many families of missing people with his charity, thank you for talking to me and sharing your thoughts and experiences. Also a special thank you to Ann Boyle for talking to me about her missing twin sister Mary. I truly hope that one day you get the answers you deserve.

To the families of Bernadette Connolly, Fiona Sinnott, Fiona Pender, Deirdre Jacob, Annie McCarrick, Ciara Breen, Trevor Deely, and anyone else who is mentioned or missing and mentioned in the book, I hope that one day you will find out what happened to your loved ones.

I would like to say a thank you to the families and those who I have mentioned in the book, including survivors of sexual abuse, who have been affected by such heinous crimes.

A huge thank you also to the former members of An Garda Siochana who spoke to me about their involvement in the case. In particular, I would like to say a special thank you to former Detective Sergeant Tom Doyle, who headed the investigation from 1998 to 2016, and whose determination to help the Cairns family get the answers they deserve has never stopped, despite now being retired. Thank you for all your invaluable help and insight.

I would also like to extend my heartfelt appreciation to the following retired officers who gave me their endless time. Former Detective Alan Bailey, Detective Inspector Gerry O'Carroll (retired), and Detective Garda John Harrington (retired).

A special thank you to Siobhan Kennedy-McGuinness, whose bravery and strength to expose her abuser Eamon Cooke I found truly inspiring.

And also to the people who shared their experiences with me while writing this book, James Dillon, Graham Callaghan, Richard Kavanagh, Kevin Branigan, I thank you very much. To Catherine Hassett, who found the teenager's schoolbag with her friend Orla, thank you for sharing the events of the evening in question for the first time.

To Nikita Cooke, thank you for having the strength and trust in me to share your story. I really appreciate it.

To the people who have shared information with me, but who did not wish to be named for their own personal reasons, thank you.

To experts in their fields who took the time to share their thoughts on the case, Dr Mark Perlin, Professor John O'Keeffe and Dr Julian Boon. Thank you to each and every one of you.

I would also like to thank my many friends in journalism who have shown great support and offered incredible advice to me along the way while writing this book. A special thank you to Barry Cummins, Niamh O'Connor, my editor and friend

# ACKNOWLEDGEMENTS

Sylvia Pownall, Conor Feehan, Brighid McLaughlin and Paul Williams.

Thank you to Steve Hanrahan and Paul Dove at Mirror Books for giving me the opportunity to write this book and for all of your help and guidance. And to Chris Sherrard for your support during the process. I would also like to say a very special thank you to Harri Aston for doing such a spectacular job editing the book, for all the invaluable advice throughout the process. It was very much appreciated.

On a personal note I would like to thank the many people, both family and friends, who have been extremely supportive while I have been working on the book.

Many thanks to Liz Clifford, Robert McMenamy, Brian Connery, bookworm John Griffin, the Nolan family, the Keleghan and Kinsella's. And a special note of appreciation to those who have always encouraged and supported me, Sharon Keleghan, Clare Keleghan, Lara O'Gorman, Niamh O'Gorman, Jacinta McMenamy, Mairead O'Gorman, Karen Doyle, Clare Nolan and Nancy McMenamy.

A very special thank you to my incredible mother Cathryn, who has always encouraged, supported and inspired me and continues to daily. To Jimmy and Ger Doyle, my second family, thank you for your endless love, encouragement and support.

To my beautiful little boy Adam, thank you for your endless hugs while writing this book, you inspire me daily and I love you very much. And finally, a very special thank you to Elaine for all your encouragement, love, support and endless advice and without whom I could not have completed this book.

*Emma McMenamy, 2021*

# USEFUL CONTACT NUMBERS AND EMAIL ADDRESSES

*If you have been affected by any of the subjects referenced in this book please reach out to one of the many services which is available.*

*If any of the sexual abuse aspects of the book have affected you and you require help there are a number of organisations you can contact including the Dublin Rape Crisis Centre on 1800 77 8888 or One In Four on 01 6624070.*

*If you have any knowledge concerning any missing person you can also call the National Missing Persons Helpline on 1890 442552.*

*If you have any information whatsoever surrounding Philip's case or any of those mentioned, please contact your local garda station or the Garda Confidential telephone number on 1800 666 111.*

*If you do not feel comfortable doing so you can email me at findingphilip1986@gmail.com, and I will gladly pass on any information to authorities or the family of those mentioned.*